IAN FLEMING : A ⎯⎯⎯⎯⎯ ⎯⎯
OF A COLLECTION

A preliminary to a bibliography

IAIN CAMPBELL

Iain Campbell, 22 Gambier Terrace, Liverpool 1.

Foreword

James Bond will celebrate his silver jubilee this year. Although Casino Royale, the first James Bond book, was published on 13th April 1953, no attempt has yet been made to produce a bibliography or checklist of Fleming's writings. I hope that this catalogue will encourage this to be done, since in it I have provided bibliographical descriptions of the major Fleming first editions, listed all the publications of which I am aware, and have also provided the more important references to criticism and Flemingiana. Items not in the collection but sufficiently important to merit a mention are shown in square brackets; the major omission from the catalogue is a checklist of Fleming's contributions to the Sunday Times: I decided that it would be too large an undertaking to include such a checklist in a catalogue of this nature. I have instead included a checklist of the second most important Fleming periodical contributions, etc. in the checklist of the Spectator in Appendix 2.

The collection is deliberately concentrated on the period to 1965, the year after Fleming's death, and usually only the more important items, often relating to films, are included after that date, although I have not been able to resist the temptation of grasping at any minor post 1965 items which have come my way.

I have not mentioned scarcity in the catalogue, which is possibly a controversial subject where the publications concerned are neither limited in number nor more than twenty-five years old. Sable Basilisk (11007C1) however must be scarce, as it is limited to about half a dozen copies. The limited edition of On Her Majesty's Secret Service and the first edition of Casino Royale in dustwrapper are difficult; many leading booksellers are currently seeking copies of Casino Royale, indeed Maggs Bros were optimistically advertising for three such copies for a great part of last year. Proof copies and signed copies are also difficult; Fleming does not appear to have been generous with his signature – there was no real need for this, and as a book collector he seems to have been well aware of its value. Three of the books containing introductions by Fleming are not easy to find in fine condition: The Education of a Poker Player, The Seven Deadly Sins and All Night at Mr Stanyhurst's; like many children's books, the first edition of Chitty Chitty Bang Bang is not easily found complete in three volumes in fine condition.

Certain of the periodicals may become hard to find; popular periodicals can often be elusive, although Playboy must have sufficient ardent conservationists to keep most Fleming enthusiasts happy. Defective copies of Playboy are common; the centre double page pin up is often missing, as are other attractive photographs. It is interesting that Playboy in the early 1960s had a status probably midway between the Tit-Bits and The Strand Magazine of seventy years earlier, which were the chosen vehicles for popularising Sherlock Holmes. Certain other periodicals, such as The Spectator and Punch, have probably not yet been destroyed in sufficient quantities by their subscribers to create a shortage. The Sunday Times Colour Section may prove difficult for future collectors, but fortunately Fleming contributed to the first issue, which like many first issues retained for their curiosity value is relatively easy to find.

The early Pan paperback editions may soon prove difficult, because they are not easily found in good condition and the vogue for collecting paperback covers has helped to destroy a large number. The paperback editions form an interesting subject bibliographically in themselves; variants are almost common and the publication of texts in covers of a different date is not infrequent (*see* 11007G2-6). I have not attempted to collect every impression of the paperbacks, but have only tried to obtain a copy of each major, if not minor, variation or variant of cover design. Neither has an attempt been made to collect the foreign editions of Fleming; I have bought a few secondhand copies on my annual pilgrimages to fly kites in Greece, and thus obtained a copy of the majority of American and French titles, but only the occasional rather unrepresentative titles in German, Swedish, Greek and Turkish.

Fleming's activities as a book collector, a journalist and an author are reflected in the collection, although naturally the major part of the collection relates to his writing, which resulted in a popular phenomenon possibly matched only by Sherlock Holmes in the field of fiction and by the Beatles in contemporary times. I believe that the collection is not only of value to the student of this phenomenon but also, for example, to the student of popular periodicals. A brief glance at the index of periodicals quickly reveals names that have vanished from the newspaper counters, whilst the transition from Lilliput 1953 to Playboy 1964 to Men Only 1976 is perhaps more than revealing.

Much of the joy of collecting Flemingiana lies in the fun in collecting the by-products of the James Bond craze — toys, film posters, jigsaw puzzles, gramophone records, the variety is great and the knowledge of the sheer impossibility of collecting every item does not detract from the enjoyment of this slightly unusual lighthearted form of collecting. This then is only a representative collection: I hope that the catalogue will prove to fellow collectors to be much more than a 'Look what I've got that you haven't got' catalogue, and will also help to open new fields for collectors and to provide important information for the student of Fleming and the cult of James Bond.

Contents

Explanations

The items in the collection are coded as follows.

1. The sectional number e.g. 9 for Thunderball, 23 for Quite Like James Bond.
2. 007 – a common denominator.
3. The class in a section e.g. E for Book Reviews, H for Foreign edition, but where a lower case letter is used the item refers to something in that class, although the item itself is not actually in the class, e.g. a bookseller's catalogue referring to a proof copy.
4. The number in the class; items are numbered in date order.
5. A few items have a double 00 suffix indicating that they are not in the collection.

Example 13007D300

   13 = The Man With the Golden Gun
   007 = common denominator
   D = Anthology, Serialisation
   3 = Number of item in date order in class
   00 = Item not in collection.

Each Section is categorised into the following classes

A. First Editions.

B. Proof Copies, inscribed copies, etc.

C. Source Material, background material, etc.

D. Anthologies and Serials.

E. Book reviews.

F. U.K. Book clubs.

G. U.K. Paperbacks.

H. Foreign Editions.

J. Films.

K. Film Reviews.

L. Miscellaneous.

Items with 00 suffix in square brackets are not in the collection.
Items with X suffix are present in collection as Xerox copies only.

References cited relate to the page numbers of the books concerned.

Amis	30007A5
Bond	26007A17
Bond Affair	30007A18
Brosnan	33007A2
Connolly	31007A7
Gant	26007A4
Lilly Library	22007A14
Pearson	26007A5
Ziegler	26007A3

A. FIRST EDITIONS

1007A1   Cr. 8vo p224 10s6d net 13.Apr 1953. Jonathan Cape. 1st edn.
Black cloth with red heart on front cover, titled in red on spine.
(Lacks d/w (nine red hearts, titled in yellow) devised by Fleming
— *see* 31007A7.)*

1007A2   2nd impr of 1007A1 1953.*

B. PROOF COPIES, ETC.

1007b1   **G.F. Sims (Rare Books) Book Catalogue 67** Summer 1967. Hurst,
Reading. Item 100: Pre-publication 1st edition inscribed to John
Hayward with his corrections £85.
Item 101 is a similar copy of Live and Let Die £50.

(*See* 22007A9 **Charles Graves: None but the Rich**)

D. ANTHOLOGIES ETC.

1007D1   **The Spy's Bedside Book** ed. **Grahame Greene and Hugh Greene.**
Rupert Hart-Davis 1957 1st edn.
pp182-184 "Blanc de Blanc Brut, 1943" (Casino Royale)
also p219 Vodka with Pepper (Moonraker)
      pp86-7 Foreign Travel (From Russia With Love)
Brief reference to Bond and Fleming p12 of introduction.
(Two Peter Fleming items are also included in this anthology)

1007D2   **The Spy's Bedside Book.** New English Library Four Square
Edition 1st reprint June 1962 wraps.

1007D3   **Gilt-Edged Bonds** with an introduction by Paul Gallico. The
Macmillan Co. New York 1961 1st printing. contains:
      Casino Royale (176pp)
      From Russia With Love (253pp)
      Dr No (256pp)
Introduction pp v-xvi includes brief biography of Fleming
(*see* 13007E2, 32007A10)

1007d4   **The New York Times Book Review** Section 7 July 30 1961 p17.
Review of 1007D3 by Anthony Boucher.

---

*(1007A1-2) Second and Third 'impressions' of Casino Royale appeared in May 1953
and May 1954. It was then 'reissued' in November 1957, and 'reprinted' in 1959 and
1960. I have not seen a copy of the November 1957 reissue, but I have copies of the
1959 and 1960 reprints. The main difference between the 1959 reprint and the 1953
impressions is the dustwrapper, which by 1959 was designed by Pat Marriott. It consists
of a Queen of Hearts (or Spades when held upside down) design of a girl in evening
clothes holding a raised champagne glass in her right hand and an O.H.M.S. letter in her
left hand; (she is **not** dressed as Vesper Lynd for the casino). The front and backstrip of
the dustwrapper have an emerald green background; a Hearts and Spades motif appears
at the head of the backstrip of the dustwrapper, which is titled in red and black on the
front and black and white on the backstrip.

The binding of the book is unchanged, and, although the printers have changed to
Lowe and Brydon (Printers) Ltd., there is no change to the layout of the text. A printer's
error of 'neard' for 'heard' on p34 has crept in, which is not corrected in the 1960
reprint. Certain signatures appear which are not in the 1953 copies. I have not traced
any textual changes.

E. BOOK REVIEWS (of 1007A1)

1007E1   **The Spectator** 17 April 1953 p494 Review by R.D. Charques

1007E2   **Punch** 6 May 1953 p558 Review by F.W.

1007E3   **The New Statesman and Nation** 9 May 1953 pp557-8 Review by J.D. Scott

1007E4   **Lilliput** May-June 1953 p109 Short review

       (Also reviewed in Sunday Times, Observer, Listener, T.L.S., Daily Telegraph, Manchester Guardian & W.H. Smith Trade News etc.)

G. PAPERBACKS (U.K.)

[1007G100   7 x 4⅜ ins. p160 2s. 18. Apr 1955 Pan Books Ltd.]

1007G2   4th printing 1959. Great Pan. Front Wrap by Peff

1007G3   10th printing 1962. Great Pan. Front Wrap of Vesper Lynd with torture scene background.

1007G4   12th printing 1962. Great Pan. Different front endpaper.

1007G5   13th printing 1963. Photo Ian Fleming rear wrap.

1007G6   18th printing 1964. Front Wrap of cheque and cards.

1007G7   22nd printing 1965. No price on front wrap.

1007G8   22nd printing 1965. Variant double printing of cheque on front wrap.

H. FOREIGN EDITIONS

1007H1   Albert Bonniers Forlag, Stockholm. 1955. Wraps. Partly unopened, with a card stating that this copy is believed to have come from Fleming's own library.

1007H2   A Signet Book (NAL) 6th Printing Oct 1962 Wraps (U.S.A.) Photo Fleming with pistol on rear wrap, 7 titles of novels shown.

       (1st U.S.A. publication Macmillan Co. 23 March 1954: paperback under title 'Too Hot to Handle' — Pearson 257).*

1007H3   A Signet Book (NAL). 25th printing n.d. Wraps. (U.S.A.) Photo Fleming + cigarette rear wrap, 13 book titles shown. 007 on corner front wrap.

1007H4   **Casino Royal.** Plon. March 1965. Wraps. (France) (Defective copy)

K. FILM REVIEWS

1007K1   **Look.** 15 November 1966 pp50-56. (U.S.A.) Article + photos 'Who is the real James Bond anyhow?'; also reference on front cover.

1007K2   **Playboy** February 1967 pp109-121. Article and photos by Woody Allen 'The Girls of Casino Royale', also references on front cover, p3 + p4.

       (Note. Fleming sold the film rights of Casino Royale in 1955, which eventually resulted in a very different James Bond film by Columbia Pictures ('a wild fantasy containing not one but *several* James Bonds!' — Brosnan 157 — 'one of the biggest box office disasters of the decade' Brosnan 158.)

---

*See Note 1, p60.

A. FIRST EDITIONS

2007A1   Cr. 8vo p224 10s6d net. 5 April 1954 Jonathan Cape. Black cloth with Edward IV gold rose noble on front cover, titled gilt on spine. 1st edn. Jacket devised by the author and executed by Kenneth Lewis, scarlet titled in yellow with rose noble on spine. *See* 1007b1 inscribed copy to John Hayward. G.F. Sims (Rare Books) Cat.67 Item 101

C. SOURCE MATERIAL

2007C1   **Patrick Leigh Fermor. Travellers Tree.** John Murray 1950. 1st edn. Long quotation from this book used by Fleming pp29-33 of 2007A1.

D. ANTHOLOGIES, ETC.

2007D1   **Best Secret Service Stories** Ed. **John Welcome.** Faber + Faber 1960 1st edn.
pp52-64 Mr Big
also references to Fleming's work pp.13-16 of introduction

2007D2   Copy of 2007D1 in Wraps. Faber + Faber 1964. 1st edition thus.

[2007D300   **More Gilt-Edged Bonds.** Also contains Moonraker and Diamonds Are Forever. (U.S.A.) (*See* 13007E2, 32007A10).]
See 23007A19 (**The James Bond Annual** 1968 Strip cartoon story reproduced by arrangement with Daily Express.)

E. BOOK REVIEW

2007E1   **Punch** 14 April 1954 p479 Review by R.G.G.P. (Price)

F. BOOK CLUB EDITION (U.K.)

2007F1   The Reprint Society Ltd. 1st edn. 1956 in Reprint Society dustwrapper.

G. PAPERBACKS (U.K.)

[2007G100   7 x 4⅜ ins. p256. 2s6d. 18 Oct 1957 Pan Books Ltd.]

2007G2   10th Printing 1963. Front Wrap of Solitaire and Bond.

2007G3   15th Printing 1964. Front Wrap of skeleton hand and coins.

H. FOREIGN EDITIONS

2007H1   A Signet Book (NAL) 7th Printing January 1963 Wraps. (U.S.A.)

2007H2   A Signet Book (NAL) 23rd Printing n.d. Wraps. (Refers to death of Fleming on rear wrap.)

2007H3   Bantam Books. U.S.A. Film edition. July 1973 Wraps.

2007H4   **Vivre et Laisser Mourir.** Plon. July 1965 Wraps. (France). (First U.S.A. publication Macmillan Co. 1955)

J. FILM

2007J1   Film Prop 27½ x 16½ ins. Card, painted in colour of The High Priestess (with letters B and J on pillars), used on set of film of Live and Let Die.

2007J2   Film Poster 40 x 30 ins. Colour. Printed by Lonsdale + Bartholomew (Nottingham) Ltd. n.d.

2007J3   **Roger Moore as James Bond.** Pan Books Ltd. 1st edn 1973. Wraps. Roger Moore's own account of filming Live and Let Die with photos by Luisa Moore and film stills.

2007J4   **Pamela Weiss** 2pp a.l.s. 17 Jan 1973 with reference to making of film in California.

2007J5   **Mayfair** Vol.9. No 5 n.d. pp102-105. Shella, Bond's Black Beauty (in film). Photos by Linzi.

2007J6   **Rex** No.9 1973 pp57-62. Bond's Date Book. Photos + captions of Roger Moore and girl from film, reference also front cover.

A. FIRST EDITIONS

3007A1   Cr. 8vo p256 10s6d. 7 April 1955. Jonathan Cape. Black cloth, titled in silver on front cover and spine. 1st edn. Jacket devised by the author and executed by Kenneth Lewis, orange, yellow and white flame design titled in black on spine and black and white on front cover.

C. SOURCE MATERIAL

3007C1   **Ely Culbertson Contract Bridge Blue Book.** The Bridge World. New York. 35th printing March 1931 (First published September 1930) Bond uses a hand devised by Culbertson to defeat Drax (Moonraker 81). The first edition of Culbertson is in the Ian Fleming Collection (Lilly Library p.27).

D. ANTHOLOGIES

3007D1   **Best Gambling Stories** ed. **John Welcome.** Faber + Faber 1961 1st edn.
pp45-65 A Game of Bridge at Blades
also reference to Fleming p.10 of introduction.

3007D2   **Argosy** (U.K. periodical) February 1962
pp71-89 A Game of Bridge at Blades

3007D3   **Motor Car Lover's Companion** ed. Richard Hough. George Allen + Unwin Ltd. 1965 1st edn.
pp256-263 Pursuit on the Dover Road

See 1007D1 (Vodka with Pepper in **The Spy's Bedside Book,** p219.
See 2007D300 (**More Gilt-Edged Bonds**)

E. BOOK REVIEWS

3007E1   **The Spectator** 22 April 1955 p512 Review by John Metcalf
3007E2   **The Tablet** 23rd April 1955 pp399-400, Review by John Biggs-Davison.
3007E3   **Punch** 27 April 1955 p537 Review by J.B.B. (Boothroyd).
3007E4   **Lilliput** June 1955 p63. Short review.

See also 16007E3 (**John O'London's.** 25 February 1960 p235).

G. PAPERBACKS (U.K.)

[**3007G100**   7 x 4⅜ ins. p192 2s. 15 October 1956 Pan Books Ltd.]
3007G2   7th printing 1961. Front wrap of Gala Brand and Bond.
3007G3   11th printing 1963. Bond's picture not at foot of front wrap.
3007G4   17th printing 1964. Front wrap of rocket.
3007G5   22nd printing 1965. Front wrap of rocket. Different f.e.p. and adverts.
3007G6   24th printing 1969. Front wrap of rocket and Gala Brand.
3007G7   26th printing 1973. Front wrap of cards, cigarette case, knife, etc.

H. FOREIGN EDITIONS

3007H1   Signet Books (NAL) 21st printing. n.d. Wraps.

3007H2   **Son Koz.** Basah Yayinevi. Istanbul. 3rd printing March 1967. Wraps.

        (First U.S.A. edition Macmillan Co. 1955)

A. FIRST EDITIONS

4007A1   Cr. 8vo. p256. 12s.6d. 26 March 1956 Jonathan Cape. Black cloth with baguette cut diamond in silver on blindstamped repeated diamond pattern on front cover, titled in silver on spine. 1st edn. Jacket design by Pat Marriott, black, white, orange and pink, of girl's V shaped neckline with solitaire pear-shaped diamond pendant on front cover, titled in white and pink on front cover and spine.*

4007A2   4th impr 1962. Similar jacket to 4007A1 and designer's name given. (Substitution of 'Windy' for 'Boofy' p134. Pearson 280.)*

(Serialised in Daily Express)

C. SOURCE MATERIAL

4007C1   **Tommy Armour. How to Play Your Best Golf All the Time.** Hodder + Stoughton 1954. 1st edn. Read by James Bond in Chapter 6 of Diamonds Are Forever (*see* also Pearson 252).

D. ANTHOLOGIES, ETC.

See 2007D300 (**More Gilt-Edged Bonds**).

E. BOOK REVIEWS

4007E1   **The Spectator** 6 April 1956 p462 + 464 − Review by John Russell. p446 Advertisement for book.

4007E2   **The New Statesman and Nation** 14 April 1956 pp380 + 382. Review by Ralph Partridge, also Advertisement for the book p385.

4007E3   **The New York Times Book Review** Section 7 28 October 1956 p22. Review by Anthony Boucher.

4007e4   **The London Magazine** Vol 3 No 5 May 1956 p84. Advertisement for book.

F. BOOK CLUB EDITIONS (U.K.)

4007F1   The Thriller Book Club. n.d. (Jacket design by Pat Marriott as 4007A1.) ('Windy' not 'Boofy')

G. PAPERBACKS (U.K.)

4007G100   7 x 4⅜ ins. p192 2s6d. 15 August 1958 Pan Books Ltd. Front wrap of Tiffany Cafe.

4007G2   2nd printing 1958 Great Pan. Front wrap of Tiffany Case.

4007G3   9th printing 1962 Great Pan. Front wrap of Tiffany Case at dressing table Price 2s6d.

4007G4   10th printing 1963 Pan Books. Front wrap of Tiffany Case at dressing table Price 3s6d.

---

*(4007A1-2) The contents are misnumbered on the Contents Page of 4007A1 by two pages from Chapter XV onwards. This error also occurs in the Book Club edition (4007F1), but is corrected in 4007A2.

4007G5	17th printing 1964. Front wrap of diamond. No price.
4007G6	18th printing 1964. Front wrap of diamond. Price 3/6.
4007G7	25th printing 1972. Film version front wrap.
4007G8	Triad/Panther Books 1977 1st thus.

H. FOREIGN EDITIONS

[4007H100	Macmillan Co. Oct 1956 $2.75. 1st U.S.A. edition.]
4007H2	A Signet Book. (NAL) 23rd printing n.d. Wraps.
4007H3	**Diamantenfieber.** Ullstein Bücher, West Berlin 1965. Wraps.

J. FILM

4007J1	**James Bond; Diamonds Are Forever.** Film Brochure. ed. **Peter Tipthorp.** Sackville Publishing Co. n.d. (1972) 24pp. Many photos. Includes article by Roderick Mann 'The Incredible World of Ian Fleming'.
4007J2	Record 33$\frac{1}{3}$ r.p.m. of film sound track. United Artists Music UAS 29216. n.d.
4007J3	Film Still (colour) 8 x 10 ins. Kidd's kebabs in brandy flames.

K. FILM REVIEWS

4007K1	**Photoplay Film Monthly** June 1971 pp14-15. Article by E.L. + photos. 'Connery Back to Bond'.
4007K2	**Photoplay Film Monthly** September 1971 pp22-24. William Hall. 'Photoplay goes on location with Bond in Las Vegas'. Many photos, also ref. front cover.
4007K3	**New Statesman** 7 January 1972 p25. Review by John Coleman.
4007K4	**Photoplay Film Monthly** March 1972 p26. Review by Betty Jennings + photos.
4007K5	**Films Illustrated** September 1973 (U.S.A.) p98. Review by Mark Whitman of 4007J2.

A. FIRST EDITIONS

5007A1   Cr. 8vo p256 13s6d. 8 Apr 1957 Jonathan Cape. Black cloth with silver modified Smith + Wesson .38 revolver with sawn off barrel and with red rose on front cover, titled in red and silver on spine. 1st edn. Jacket devised by the author and executed by Richard Chopping with similar revolver and red rose design, titled in black on front cover and spine.

5007A2   7th impr. 1963.

          (Serialised in Daily Express)

B. PROOF COPY

5007B1   Uncorrected Proof Copy of 5007A1. Wraps. Pencil notes on four of blank pages at end for a review by John Raymond in New Statesman 27 April 1957 (*See* 5007E2 below). Publishers blurb Spring List 1957 on verso front wrap.*

C. SOURCE MATERIAL, ETC.

5007C1   **Sunday Times** 25th November 1973 p.12 Newscutting article by Rosemary Righter headed 'Russian bid for forgotten tunnel' stating that conduit between Russian embassy and Kensington barracks was transposed by Fleming to Istanbul in From Russia With Love.

5007C2   **Eric Ambler: The Mask of Dimitrios.** Hodder + Stoughton 1939. 1st edition. Read by James Bond in Chapter 13 of From Russia With Love.

5007C3   **Michael Barsley: Orient Express.** The Story of the World's Most Fabulous Train. Macdonald 1966 1st edn. Many references to Ian Fleming and From Russia With Love (also reference on dust-wrapper). *See* also 30007A18.

D. ANTHOLOGIES, ETC.

          See 1007D1 (Foreign Travel in **The Spy's Bedside Book** pp86-87)
          See 1007D3 (**Gilt-Edged Bonds**).

E. BOOK REVIEWS, ETC.

5007E1   **The Spectator** 12 April 1957 Review by Anthony Hartley

5007E2   **The New Statesman and Nation** 27 April 1957 p536 Review by John Raymond entitled 'The Late James Bond'.

5007E3   **Life** 17 March 1961 U.S.A. edition. pp55-60. The President's Voracious Reading Habits by Hugh Sidey. p59 Reference to Fleming: From Russia With Love is shown in list of Ten Kennedy Favorites. This article caused a tremendous upsurge in popularity of Bond books in U.S.A. (Pearson 327, Bond 21, Bond Affair 17) (*But see* 31007A1).

---

*See Note 2, p60.

F. BOOK CLUB EDITION (U.K.)

5007F1   The Book Club. n.d. Jacket design by Richard Chopping (as 5007A1).

5007F2   Variant of 5007F1 with title page of Jonathan Cape 1st edition.

G. PAPERBACKS (U.K.)

[5007G100   7 x 4⅜ p208 2s6d 10 April 1959. Pan Books Ltd. Front Wrap of Orient Express, Tatiana Romanova + Bond.]

5007G2   2nd Printing 1959 Great Pan. Front Wrap of Orient Express, Tatiana Romanova + Bond.

5007G3   9th Printing 1962 Great Pan. Front Wrap of Tatiana Romanova + Orient Express.

5007G4   12th Printing 1963 Pan Books. Front Wrap of Tatiana Romanova + Orient Express. Price now 3s6d.

5007G5   12th Printing 1963 Pan Books. Film Version front wrap + new prelims.

5007G6   19th Printing 1965. Front Wrap of Faberge Coronation Egg. No Price. 'The End' at end.

5007G7   20th Printing 1965. Front Wraps as 5007G6 Price 3/6. No 'The End' at end of text.

5007G8   25th Printing 1974. Front Wrap of Turkish items.

5007G9   Triad/Panther Books 1977 1st thus.

H. FOREIGN EDITIONS

5007H1   A Signet Book (NAL) 23rd Printing n.d. Wraps.

5007H2   **Bons Baisers de Russie.** Plon. 1964. Wraps. (1st edn 4½ x 7 p311 Barmerlea March 1964).

5007H3   Another copy of 5007H2 with variant backstrip and 3 film adverts on f.e.p. March 1965.

5007H4   **Kamrat Mordare.** Zebra Special. Albert Bonniers Forlag, Stockholm. 1965. Wraps.
(First U.S.A. publication Macmillan Co. 1957)

J. FILM

5007J1   Film Still (colour) 8 x 10 ins. Rosa Klebb interviewing Tatiana Romanova

5007J2   Film Still (b/w) 8 x 10 ins. Rosa Klebb and Red Grant. (Brosnan 37)

5007J3   Film Still (b/w) 8 x 10 ins. James Bond with gipsy girl.

K. FILM REVIEWS

5007K1   **The Spectator** 18 October 1963 pp495-6 Review by Isabel Quigly.

5007K2   **Punch** 23 October 1963 p610 Review by Richard Mallett with caricature by ffolkes.

5007K3   **Time** 10 April 1964 Atlantic edition. pp63-4. Review + photo.
(See also 33007A6-7 **007 James Bond in Focus**)

A. FIRST EDITIONS

6007A1   Cr. 8vo. p256. 13s6d. 31 March 1958 Jonathan Cape. Black cloth
          with silhouette of girl in brown on front cover, titled in silver on
          spine. 1st edn. Jacket design by Pat Marriott, black silhouette of
          girl on brown background, title in black and white on front cover
          and on spine. First novel with © Glidrose Productions Ltd.

6007A2   As 6007A1 but with plain front cover.
          Both Connolly 48 and Lilly Library 33 refer to 6007A1 as having
          the silhouette blind stamped on front cover; I believe that this
          may be an inadvertent misdescription, because I have only seen
          copies with the silhouette in brown, and on none of the copies
          has the design been impressed. Lilly Library lists both 6007A1
          and 6007A2 in that order without giving any priority, stating
          both to be first editions in variant bindings. Since Fleming there-
          fore knew of the variants and did not give one priority, one cannot
          treat 6007A1 as a first issue with any great degree of certainty.
          6007A1 is more difficult to find than 6007A2, and later impres-
          sions all have plain front covers. It thus seems that 6007A1 was
          an experiment which was not continued. Connolly refers only to
          6007A1, and apparently was unaware of the existence of 6007A2.

6007A3   6th impr. 1964 (Plain front cover).

D. ANTHOLOGIES, ETC.

6007D1   **Stag** May 1962 (U.S.A.)
          pp24-27, 84-97 'Nude Girl of Nightmare Key'. A Stag Suspense
          novel. Illustrated. Front cover headline reference also.*

          See 1007D3 **Gilt-Edged Bonds.**

E. BOOK REVIEWS

          See 21007A11 (**The Spectator** 4th April 1958 p438 Review by
          Simon Raven entitled 'Gilt-Edged Bond of Dr No') and *See also*
          16007E3 (**John O'London's** 25 February 1960 p235) and
          32007A1 (**The Twentieth Century** March 1958)

F. BOOK CLUB EDITION

6007F1   The Book Club n.d. (Jacket design Pat Marriott as 6007A1)

G. PAPERBACKS (U.K.)

6007G1   Cr. 8vo. p192 2s6d. 12 February 1960 Great Pan. Front Wrap by
          Peff. 1st thus.

6007G2   2nd Printing 1960. Same wraps, different adverts. at end.

6007G3   9th Printing 1963. Front wrap film version.

6007G4   19th Printing 1965. Front wrap of spider's web. No price.

6007G5   19th Printing 1965. Variant Front Wrap of spider's web. Price
          3s6d.

*(6007D1) A condensed version of Dr No with minor amendments for U.S. market.

6007G6	21st Printing 1970. Front Wrap of Honeychile Rider.
6007G7	23rd Printing 1973. Front Wrap of guns and white sticks.
6007G8	Printers Block 6½ x 5¾ inches backed by matt colour variant Wrap of 6007G1 with rubber stamp 'TYPE HIGH'.
6007G9	Triad/Panther Books 1977. 1st thus.

H. FOREIGN EDITIONS

6007H1	A Signet Book (NAL) 11th Printing June 1963. Reference to film on front + rear wraps.
6007H2	A Signet Book (NAL) 12th Printing Sept 1963. Wraps. No film references.
6007H3	**James Bond Contre Dr No.** Plon. Oct. 1964. Wraps (1st edn 4½ x 7 ins p310 Barmerlea March 1964). (1st U.S.A. edition Macmillan Co. 1958)

J. FILM

6007J1	E.M.I. Mono Record 33⅓ r.p.m. © 1962.
6007J2	Poster 20¾ x 13¾ ins in French. Colour. Printed in Brussels. n.d. (Belgium)
6007J3	Film Still (colour) 8 x 10 ins. Bond and Dr No's guards.
6007J4	Film Still (b/w) 8 x 10 ins. James Bond in casino. (Brosnan 16).
6007J5	Film Still (b/w) 8 x 10 ins. Honey (Ursula Andress) in bikini. (cf. Brosnan 22).
6007J6	Film Still (b/w) 8 x 10 ins. James Bond and Honey.
6007J7	Film Still (b/w) 8 x 10 ins. Ursula Andress and Ian Fleming on set of Dr No.

(See also 30007E13)

K. FILM REVIEW

6007K1	**Scene** No 4 5 October 1962 p19. Review by Derek Hill entitled 'The Infallible Dr No' with photo.
6007K2	**John O'London's** 11 October 1962 p347. Review by Peter Green with photo.
6007K3	**The Spectator** 12 October 1962 p560. Review by Ian Cameron, also p549 review of film in Spectator's Notebook, also p557 letter from J.B. Snell 'Russian Bonds'.

See also 24007A11 **Playboy** July 1966, 33007A6-7 **007 James Bond in Focus.**

A. FIRST EDITIONS

7007A1   Cr. 8vo. p320. 15s. 23 March 1959 Jonathan Cape. Black cloth with blind stamped skull and gold coins as eyes in gilt on front cover, titled gilt on spine. 1st edn. Jacket designed by Richard Chopping with skull with gold coin eyes and red rose on front cover, titled in black on front cover and spine.

7007a2   Sotheby + Co. Book Auction Sale Catalogue 15th + 16th July 1974 Lot 108 1st edn orig. dec. cloth, with price list tipped in showing lot 108 Passed.

B. PROOF COPY

7007b1   G.F. Sims (Rare Books) Book Catalogue 56 n.d. c1965 Item 231 uncorrected proof copy at £2.

C. SOURCE MATERIAL, ETC.

7007c1   Colin Harding: Canasta for All The Sunday Times. 74pp. Wraps. n.d. (c1950). Possible source material for Canasta game in Goldfinger, in view of Sunday Times connection.

7007C2   The Bible Designed to be Read as Literature. Edited and Arranged by Ernest Sutherland Bates. William Heinemann Ltd. 4th edn. n.d. (Inscr. d 1948 on e.p.). *See* Goldfinger p46 'Bond went to his suitcase again and took out a thick book − The Bible Designed to be Read as Literature − opened it and extracted his Walther PPK in the Berns Martin holster. . . .'

E. BOOK REVIEWS, ETC.

7007E1   Books and Bookmen March 1959 p9. Jacket of the Month. Photo + 6 line caption.

7007E2   Spectator 27 March 1959 p448. Review by Christopher Pym.

7007E3   Books and Bookmen April 1959 p27. Review by Brian Baumfield + brief biography of Fleming + advert for Bond Pan Books paperbacks. Also front cover photo of Ian Fleming by Douglas Glass.

7007E4   The Tablet 25 April 1959 p402 Review by Anthony Lejeune.

7007E5   Lilliput May 1959 p17 Short review.

7007E6   The Twentieth Century Magazine May 1959 p536 Review by Marjorie Bremner.

F. BOOK CLUB EDITION

7007F1   The Book Club. n.d. (Jacket by Cuthill)

G. PAPERBACK EDITIONS (U.K.)

7007G1   1st Printing Great Pan. 1961. Pan Books Ltd. Front wrap of Pussy Galore + Bond.

7007G2   2nd Printing Great Pan 1961. Variant front wrap of Pussy Galore + Bond. No price.

7007G3   11th Printing 1964. Front Wrap of Rolls Royce bonnet.

7007G4	12th Printing 1964. Front Wrap of Rolls Royce bonnet. Australia price now on rear wrap.
7007G5	15th Printing 1964. Front wrap of film version.
7007G6	18th Printing 1965. Variant wrap of film version. No price.
7007G7	23rd Printing 1973. Front wrap of tankard, camera, etc.

H. FOREIGN EDITIONS

7007H1	The Macmillan Company New York n.d. Book Club edn. (First U.S.A. edn. 1959).
7007H2	A Signet Book (NAL) 23rd Printing. n.d. Wraps.
7007H3	Plon. Feb 1965. Wraps. (1st edn 4 x 7 ins. p313 Barmerlea June 1964).

J. FILM

7007J1	Poster 22½ x 20¾ ins. Colour. In French. Printed in Brussels with times of films handwritten at top, stamped 14.6.1967 on reverse and addressed to Meur Charlier, Epicerie, Mortehan.
7007J2	Aston Martin D85 Die-cast scale model. Corgi Toys 270. Playcraft Toys Ltd. Complete in original box with secret instructions and spare villain in packet. (Connolly 47).
7007J3-4	Two smaller Aston Martin D85 Die-cast scale models. Husky. Both lacking villains and with fewer refinements than Corgi model.
7007J5	Film Still (colour) 8 x 10 ins Bond + Pussy Galore in the hay.
7007J6	Film Still (colour) 8 x 10 ins Bond + Goldfinger struggle in airliner (Brosnan 71).
7007J7	**Honor Blackman. Honor Blackman's Book of Self-Defence.** Andre Deutsch 1965 1st edn. Brief James Bond film reference in foreword and on inside dustwrapper (Goldfinger film photo on rear): really an Avengers offshoot additionally trading on Bond name.

K. FILM REVIEWS

7007K1	**Photoplay** August 1964 pp21-28. 'Bond Assignment "Goldfinger".' Preview of film by Ken Ferguson including full-page colour photos of both Honor Blackman and Sean Connery. Also front cover colour photo of Sean Connery and Shirley Eaton.
7007K2	**The Observer Colour Magazine** 6 September 1964 pp21-26. 'The Man Who Gilded Goldfinger' by Stanley Price. Photos.
7007K3	**The Spectator** 18 September 1964 p372. Review by Isabel Quigly.
7007K4	**Punch** 30 September 1964 p595. Review by Richard Mallett with caricature by Mahood.
7007K5	**Films and Filming** October 1964 p45. Photos of film, reference p27 to premiere + release of film, full page advert p6, also ref fr cover.
7007K6	**Life International** 2nd November 1964. Cover photo + pp58-61 (Defective copy).
7007K7	**Saturday Review** (U.S.A.) 12 December 1964 p42. Review by Hollis Alpert.

7007K8   **Dapper** April 1965 Vol 2 No 1 (U.S.A.) 'James Bond's Newest Girls' pp25-33 — Honor Blackman + Vicki Kennedy.

7007K9   **TV Times** Oct 30-Nov 5 1976 (ATV) Front page cover colour picture — 'Wednesday's Big Film', summary etc. p38 (photo), cast etc p61 (photos).

   See also 33007A6-7 **007 James Bond in Focus.**

A. FIRST EDITIONS

8007A1 Cr. 8vo p256 15s 11 April 1960 Jonathan Cape. Black cloth with painted eye in white on front cover, titled gilt on spine. 1st edn. Jacket design by Richard Chopping, with eye looking through hole in unpainted wooden door, titled in black and red on front cover and spine. (The only James Bond dust wrapper with a glossy surface.)

8007A2 2nd impression June 1960.

D. ANTHOLOGIES, ETC.

[8007D100 **Playboy** March 1960 The Hildebrand Rarity.]

8007D2 **To Catch a Spy** ed. **Eric Ambler.** The Bodley Head 1964 1st edn. pp181-212 From a View to Kill. (Short references to Fleming pp18+22 of Introduction.)

8007D3 Paperback version of 8007D2 A Four Square Book. 1st thus. May 1966. pp166-195.

8007D4 Paperback version of 8007D2 Fontana Books Ltd. 1st thus 1974. pp153-179.

8007D5 **Best Secret Service Stories 2.** ed. **John Welcome.** Faber + Faber 1965 1st edn. pp73-93 The Quantum of Solace Also pp9-18 Introduction, much of which concerns Fleming and his recent death.

8007D6 **The Twelfth Anniversary Playboy Reader.** ed. **Hugh M. Hefner.** Souvenir Press London 1965. Printed cellophane d/w. 1st thus. pp345-374 The Hildebrand Rarity. (also brief introduction).

8007D7 **The Playboy Book of Crime and Suspense** Souvenir Press London 1967. 1st thus. pp1-40 The Hildebrand Rarity (also brief introduction which differs from 8007D6).

8007D8 **The Best from Playboy Number Two** Playboy Press (1968). 1st thus. pp4-16 The Hildebrand Rarity. Illustrated by Allan Phillips.

E. BOOK REVIEWS

8007E1 **The Spectator** 29 April 1960 p635 Review by Christopher Pym.

8007E2 **The Tablet** 30 April 1960 p422. Review by Anthony Lejéune.

8007E3 **The Twentieth Century** August 1960 p188 Review by Marjorie Bremner.

F. BOOK CLUB EDITION

8007F1 The Book Club. n.d. (Jacket by Cuthill).

G. PAPERBACK EDITIONS (U.K.)

8007G1 Cr. 8vo p192 2s6d. 11 May 1962 Great Pan. 1st edn Pan Books Ltd. Front Wrap of Lisl Baum + notice.

8007G2	2nd Printing 1962 Great Pan. Front Wrap of Lisl Baum + notice. No price. (Sticker used).
8007G3	3rd Printing 1962 Great Pan. Front Wrap of Lisl Baum + notice. Price 2s6d (as 8007G1).
8007G4	9th Printing 1964. Front Wrap of red rubber stamp For Your Eyes Only.
8007G5	15th Printing 1965. Variant front wrap of red rubber stamp For Your Eyes Only. No price.
8007G6	19th Printing 1973. Front wrap of red rose, goggles, etc.

H. FOREIGN EDITIONS

8007H1	A Signet Book (NAL) 13th Printing August 1964 Wraps.
8007H2	**Bons Baisers de Paris.** Plon. June 1965. Wraps.
8007H3	**Cok Gizli** Basak Yayinevi, Istanbul. 1966 Wraps.
8007H4	**For Your Eyes Only: Read and Destroy** by **Louis Honig.** Bantam Books. New York Sept 1973 (1st pub Oct 1972). Wraps. Book concerning Vietnam War apparently accidentally with Fleming title.
	(First U.S.A. edition Viking Press 1960).

J. FILM

8007J1	**Screen International** 14 Jan 1978 pl Article 'Bond joins tax exiles' (principal photography of For Your Eyes Only to be abroad, mainly because of U.K. punitive tax laws).

A. FIRST EDITIONS

9007A1   Cr. 8vo. p256 15s. 27 March 1961 Jonathan Cape. Black cloth with blind stamped skeleton hand and wrist on front cover, titled gilt on spine. 1st edn. Jacket design by Richard Chopping with skeleton hand and wrist, clasp knife and playing cards, titled in black on front cover and spine.

9007A2   2nd impr. 1964.

D. ANTHOLOGIES, ETC.

[9007D100] **Argosy** December 1961 (U.S.A.) Shortened version.]

9007D2   **Now + Then** No.107. Spring 1961. (pub Jonathan Cape) p7. Operation Thunderball (Spectre letter).

E. BOOK REVIEWS

9007E1   **The Spectator** 31 March 1961 Review by Geoffrey Grigson.

9007E2   **The Tablet** 29th April 1961 p418 Review by Anthony Lejeune.

     See also 28007A10 **Now + Then**. Autumn 1960.

F. BOOK CLUB EDITION

9007F1   The Book Club n.d. (Jacket design by Cuthill).

G. PAPERBACK EDITIONS (U.K.)

9007G1   3s.6d. Pan X201 3 May 1963 1st edn Pan Books Ltd. Front wrap with bullet hole.

9007G2   12th Printing 1965. Front wrap with bullet hole, variant rear wrap with Australian price.

9007G3   13th Printing 1965. Front wrap of film version.

9007G4   14th Printing (reset) 1965. Front wrap of film version. Extra and different adverts at end.

9007G5   16th Printing 1966. Front wrap of diver's mask + watch. Price 30p (thus after Feb 1971).

9007G6   17th Printing 1973. Additional dedication page + title page.

H. FOREIGN EDITIONS

9007H1   The Viking Press New York 1961 (1st U.S.A. edn. April 1961).

9007H2   A Signet Book (NAL) 7th printing July 1963. Wraps (1st printing May 1962).

9007H3   A Signet Book (NAL) 23rd printing n.d. Wraps. Different wraps and reference to McClory and Whittingham on title page.

9007H4   **Operation Tonnere**. Plon. July 1965. Wraps.

9007H5   **Askbollen**. Zebra Special. Albert Bonniers Forlag, Stockholm 1965. Wraps.

9007H6   ΕΠΙΧΕΙΡΗΣΙΣ ΚΕΡΑΥΝΟΣ ΓΙΑΝ ΦΛΕΜΙΝΓΚ λυχναρι (1965) Wraps.

J. FILM

9007J1   **James Bond in Thunderball** Film Brochure. Sackville Publishing Ltd. 1965. 32pp. Many Photos. ed. **Peter Tipthorp**. Wraps. Contents include: Roderick Mann — The Man Who Created Bond, Jane Reynolds — A Woman's View of Bond, David Lewin — Sean Connery — The Screen's James Bond, Alexander Walker — From Dr No to Now, John Holt — Rogue's Gallery, Richard Maibaum — Writing the Bond Films, Tony Crawley — The Bond Girls, David Benson — The JB007 (car).

9007J2   As 9007J1, but substantially bound in orange cloth.

9007J3   **Ian Fleming. James Bond 007 in the Incredible World of Thunderball.** A Corgi 007. Published by Transworld Publishers Ltd. n.d. 56pp. Many photos. Wraps.

9007J3   Broadside Cinema advertisement 9 x 4½ ins. Odeon, Preston. Sun. March 27 (1966). Several copies neatly torn in half.

9007J4   Film Poster 30 x 20 ins. Printed by W.E. Berry Ltd. Bradford n.d.

9007J6   Film Poster. **Operation Tonnere.** 24¼ x 19½ ins. In French. Colour. Printed in Brussels.

9007J7   Film Still (colour) 8 x 10 ins. Bond in underwater suit checking his watch.

K. FILM REVIEW

9007K1   **Courier** Vol 44 No 4 April 1965 p62 Sidney Vauncez. 'The Cost of Crime': includes two paragraphs on the £2m cost of filming Thunderball.

9007K2   **The Spectator** 31 December 1965 pp864-5. Review by Isabel Quigly.

9007K3   **John O'London's** April 1966 p10. Brief reference.

See also 23007A19 **The James Bond 007 Annual.**

A. FIRST EDITIONS

10007A1 Cr. 8vo p224 15s. April 1962 Jonathan Cape. Black cloth with blind stamped Wilkinson dagger with silver blade on front cover, titled in silver on spine 1st edn. Jacket design by Richard Chopping with Wilkinson dagger, red carnation, burnt paper and burnt matchstick design on front cover, titled in black on front cover and spine.

10007A2 Another copy of 10007A1. Space not pushed down between E and M of Fleming on title page.

10007A3 6th impr March 1964

10007A4 7th impr March 1965*

E. BOOK REVIEWS

10007E1 **The Times Literary Supplement** 20 April 1962 p261.

10007E2 **The Tablet** 28 April 1962 p403 Review by Anthony Lejeune.

10007E3 **New Statesman** 11 May 1962 p684 Review by G.W. Stonier.

10007E4 **The Spectator** 1 June 1962 pp728-9 Review by Esther Howard.

F. BOOK CLUB EDITION

10007F1 The Book Club n.d. (Jacket design by Cuthill.)

G. PAPERBACK EDITIONS (U.K.)

10007G1 Pan Books Ltd. 1st Printing 1967. Front wrap of U.S. road map.

10007G2 7th printing 1972. Front wrap of Vivienne Michel + Sluggsy. (Note: the last James Bond item to appear in paperback in U.K.)

H. FOREIGN EDITIONS

10007H1 The Viking Press. New York. n.d. (First U.S.A. edn 1962).

10007H2 A Signet Book (NAL) 16th Printing. n.d. Wraps. Price increase label front wrap.

10007H3 A Signet Book (NAL) 17th Printing. No price increase label front wrap.

10007H4 Motel 007. Plon. n.d. (1966). Wraps.

J. FILM

10007J1 Ticket Application Form, etc., for Royal Charity Premiere (Princess Anne) of The Spy Who Loved Me. 7 July 1977.

10007J2 Film Still (b/w) 8 x 10 ins. Diagram of 007 submarine car.

---

*(10007A4) The front cover of the first edition measures the standard James Bond size of 195 x 123mm, but the seventh impression, the first to be bound by Butler and Tanner Ltd., measures only 190 x 122mm. The page size is also reduced by 5mm in height, but the binding and printing are unchanged. It is therefore in one sense the shortest of the James Bond novels.

K. FILM REVIEWS, ETC.

10007K1   **Sunday Express** 15 August 1976 p2. Leading item in 'Town Talk' by Peter McKay. 'My Goodness What a fuss over James Bond's Leading Lady'. (pp1-2 only)

10007K2   **Daily Mail** 29 July 1976. Newscutting. Roderick Gilchrist: 'Bond Film Men spend £1½m on new studio'.

10007K3   **Sunday Express** 31 October 1976 p23. Roderick Mann: 'The film that Ian Fleming didn't want made'. Photo Barbara Bach. (pp23-24 only)

10007K4   **Daily Mirror** 6 December 1976 p3. Photo of seven scantily clad girls from film entitled 'The Mirror presents Bond's assets stripped DOUBLE OOH! SEVEN! (pp3+4 only)

10007K5   **The Times** 28 March 1977 p11. Article with photo 'James Bond's New Music Man' re Marvin Hamlisch who wrote the theme for the film. (newscutting only)

10007K6   **Photoplay Film Monthly** April 1977 pp30-31, 54. 'Roger Moore tells Roy Pickard on the set of 'The Spy Who Loved Me'; pp32-33 + front wrap 'Bond's Bosom Pals in "The Spy Who Loved Me" '; p8 photo of Roger Moore and of Sean Connery both in Arab headdress.

10007K7   **Career** Vol 10 No 1 1977. Cover photograph is a colour still from the film of The Spy Who Loved Me

(*See also* 23007A24 **Christopher Wood; James Bond, The Spy Who Loved Me.** The Book of the Film)

(A White plastic James Bond car by Corgi Toys has been produced which is based on 10007J2.)

A. FIRST EDITIONS

11007A1   Cr. 8vo p288 16s. 1963. Jonathan Cape. Black boards with white ski track design on front cover, titled in silver on spine 1st edn. Jacket design by Richard Chopping with artist's hands completing design of Bond coat of arms on front cover, titled in red and black on front cover and spine. Amherst Villiers portrait of Fleming on jacket.

11007A2   2nd impr. April 1963.

11007A3   7th impr. 1964 (extra titled on ½ title verso and rear d/w and amendment of reference to film of From Russia With Love on rear d/w)

B. PROOF COPIES, ETC.

[11007B100 Edition of 250 numbered copies printed on special paper with frontispiece portrait by Amherst Villiers and signed by the author.]

11007b2   **G.F. Sims (Rare Books)** Book Catalogue 61 n.d. (c1965) Item 124. One of special issue of 250 copies priced at £5.

11007b3   **G.F. Sims (Rare Books)** Book Catalogue 62 Autumn 1965 Item 247. Uncorrected Proof Copy priced at £5 (also Item 248 Uncorrected Proof Copy of The Man With The Golden Gun, priced at £4.4.-.)

C. SOURCE MATERIAL

11007C1   **Sable Basilisk** Notes and Correspondence between Robin de la Lanne-Mirrlees and Fleming 51pp 1960-1964. Inscribed 'Private + Confidential – Best wishes from Sable Basilisk'. Xerox type copies typescript bound in buckram in buckram slip case. Note: OHMSS is dedicated 'For Sable Basilisk Pursuivant and Hilary Bray who came to the aid of the party'.

11007c2   Letter 10 May 1974 from Robin de la Lanne Mirrlees stating that there are only about half a dozen copies of Sable Basilisk in existence.

11007c3   Fifteen eighteenth and nineteenth century heraldic bookplates of persons named Bond, many showing the correct Bond family motto in Latin 'Non sufficit orbis' instead of the English translation given by Robin de la Lanne-Mirrlees and used on the dust-wrapper of On Her Majesty's Secret Service (also *see* p71). On one bookplate is a more suitable Bond motto 'Nihil ultra vires'.

11007c4   Nineteenth century heraldic bookplate of Rev Thomas Calthorpe Blofeld of Norfolk (1777-1855). The use of Blofeld as an English surname was not apparently traced by Robin de la Lanne Mirrlees and thus no reference to this unsuitable possible ancestor of Fleming's villain appears in On Her Majesty's Secret Service.

11007c5   **James and Jeannette Riddell. Ski Holiday in the Alps** Penguin Books 1961. 1st edn. Provides useful contemporary information about the Alpine Ski scene including modern spelling of the village to which Bond ski-ed Samedan (not Samaden) – probably not therefore consulted by Fleming.

D. ANTHOLOGIES, ETC. – Serialisation

11007D1   **Playboy** April 1963 pp70-74, 162-186. Part I illus by Robert Weaver.*

11007D2   **Playboy** May 1963 pp88-90, 114-116, 170-195 Part II.

11007D3   **Playboy** June 1963 pp114-116, 136, 140-163 (Final Part). Also references on all issues front cover, p3 + p4, and on penultimate page of April + May issues.

11007d4   **Playboy** July 1963 p7 letters headed 'Bond's Men' re OHMSS serialisation etc.

E. BOOK REVIEWS

11007E1   **New Statesman** 5 April 1963. p497. Review by Brigid Brophy.

11007E2   **The Spectator** 26 April 1963 p544. Review by Antonia Sandford and p540 advertisement for the book.

        See 32007A5X re inaccuracies in this book.

11007E3   **The Spectator** 19 July 1963 p82. Letter from Francis Searson confirming correct detail re Pol Roger Champagne half bottles in this book.

11007E4   **The British Ski Year Book 1963** Vol XX No 44 p259. Review pointing out a few technical faults (Amis 117)

        (*See also* 13007C1 Allen Dulles. The Craft of Intelligence)

F. BOOK CLUB EDITION

11007F1   The Book Club. n.d. (Jacket Design by Cuthill)

G. PAPERBACK EDITIONS (U.K.)

[11007G100 Pan Books Ltd. 1st edn 1964.]

11007G2   4th printing 1955. Front Wrap of ring and blood on snow.

11007G3   4th printing 1965. Variant front wrap of film version with f.e.p. + dedication page. Decimal price shown in brackets, film released 1970, likely date thus 1970/71.

11007G4   6th printing 1965. Front Wrap as 11007G2 but no price, probably predates 11007G3.

11007G5   6th printing 1965. Front Wrap of ski equipment and gun, has dedication page but no f.e.p. Decimal price, thus post February 1971.

11007G6   7th printing 1972. Front Wrap as 11007G5, Decimal price, has f.e.p. but no dedication page.

11007G7   Triad/Panther Books 1977. 1st thus.

H. FOREIGN EDITIONS

11007H1   A Signet Book (NAL) 10th printing n.d. Wraps.

11007H2   **Au Service Secret De Sa Majeste**. Plon. 1964. Wraps (1st edn 4 x 7 p252 Barmerlea Feb 1964)

        (First U.S.A. edition New American Library 1963)

---

*(11007D1-3, 12007D1-4, 13007D1-4) Slightly shortened version of the first edition with minor amendments for U.S. market.

J. FILM

11007J1   Colour Poster 40 x 30 ins. Printed by Lonsdale + Bartholomew (Nottingham) Ltd.

11007J2   Film Still (b/w) 8 x 10 ins. Blofeld (Telly Savalas) and cat. (Brosnan 121)

K. FILM REVIEWS

11007K1   **Films and Filming** September 1969 pp10-11. Picture Preview (also Harry Salzman interview pp5-7)

11007K2   **Photoplay Film Monthly** January 1970 pp16-19 + 29. Ken Johns-Lazenby: '007 Bond On Her Majesty's Secret Service'. Preview of Film. Photos. Ref on front cover.

A. FIRST EDITIONS

12007A1   Cr. 8vo p256 16s. 16 March 1964 Jonathan Cape. Black cloth, titled in silver on spine and Japanese characters in gilt on front cover. 1st edn. Jacket Design by Richard Chopping with toad, dragonfly and pink chrysanthemum design on front cover, titled in black on front cover and spine. (Connolly 65 inexplicably refers to Chinese characters instead of Japanese characters on front cover)*

12007A2   2nd impression April 1964.

C. SOURCE MATERIAL

12007C1   **James Kirkup: These Horned Islands** Collins 1962 1st edn. Lilly Library p39 quotes Fleming's reference to and strong recommendation of this book, Meeting with Japan, and Hekura; The Diving Girl's Island by Fosco Maraini, and The Heart of Japan by Alexander Campbell.

12007C2   **Fosco Maraini: Meeting with Japan** Hutchinson + Co. 2nd impr in G.B. Sept 1959 (1st impr Sept 1959). *See* 12007C1 above.

D. ANTHOLOGIES, ETC. – Serialisation

12007D1   **Playboy** April 1964 pp70-76, 128, 131, 134-5, 138-156 Part I. Illus. Daniel Schwarz. Also p136, 'Sean Connery Scotland's gilt-edged Bond', photo.†

12007D2   **Playboy** May 1964 pp78-80, 112, 152-178 Part II.

12007D3   **Playboy** May 1964 (USA edn)

12007D4   **Playboy** June 1964 pp100-102, 108, 173, 184 Conclusion. Also references on all issues front cover, p3 + p4, and on penultimate page of April + May issues.

See also 15007D1

E. BOOK REVIEWS

12007E1   **The Spectator** 20 March 1964 p389. Review by Simon Raven; also p385 advertisement for this book.

12007E2   **The Listener** 26 March 1964 p529. Review by Maggie Ross.

12007E3   **The Tablet**. 25 April 1964 p472. Review by Anthony Lejeune.

See also 17007E4 **Courier** April 1964.

F. BOOK CLUB EDITION

12007F1   The Book Club n.d. (Jacket Design by Cuthill)

G. PAPERBACK EDITIONS (U.K.)

[12007G100 Pan Books Ltd. 1st Printing 1965.]

12007G2   2nd Printing 1966. Front Wrap of scorpion and pearl.

12007G3   2nd Printing 1966. Variant Front Wrap of film version.

*See Note 3, p60.
† See Footnote, p23.

12007G4	2nd Printing 1966. Variant Front Wrap of lobster, cigarette holder, etc. Bound upside down. Price 30p: thus after Feb 1971.
12007G5	3rd Printing 1966. Front Wrap of scorpion and pearl. Rear ep reversal of titles.
12007G6	4th Printing. Front Wrap of lobster, cigarette holder, etc. Has f.e.p. + adverts unlike 12007G5.

H. FOREIGN EDITIONS

12007H1	New American Library Book Club edition in binding to match **Goldfinger**. n.d. (First U.S.A. edition August 1964)
12007H2	New American Library Book Club edition. In matt dust jacket.
12007H3	New American Library Book Club edition. In glossy dust jacket.
12007H4	A Signet Book (NAL) 1st Printing July 1965. Wraps.
12007H5	**On Ne Vit Que Deux Fois** Plon. Feb 1965. Wraps.

J. FILM

12007J1	Trailer Film Script. **You Only Live Twice.** Teaser Trailer. United Artists. 3-1-67. U.S.A.
12007J2	Film Script. English Release Script. Mai Harris, London. June 1967.
12007J3	Film Poster 21¼ x 14¼ ins. **On Ne Vit Que Deux Fois.** Colour. In French. Printed in Brussels.
12007J4	Film Still (colour) 8 x 10 ins. Interior scene of hollow volcano. Caption: 'Sean Connery is James Bond in Ian Fleming's "You Only Live Twice"'.
12007J5	As 12007J4 but with pasted slip amending caption to 'Sean Connery as James Bond. . . .'
12007J6	As 12007J4 but with pasted slip amending caption to 'Sean Connery in Ian Fleming's . . . .'
12007J7	Film Still (colour) 8 x 10 ins Bond dining with Kissy Suzuki (caption as 12007J6)
12007J8	Film Still (colour) 8 x 10 ins Bond with Blofeld and Cat. (Caption as 12007J6)

K. FILM REVIEWS

12007K1	**Photoplay** December 1966 pp52-53 + 57. 'Bond in Japan, William Hall goes on location with Secret Agent 007'. Photos, also front cover colour photo.
12007K2	**Playboy** June 1967 pp86-91. Roald Dahl (scriptwriter of this film) '007's Oriental Eyefuls, a pictorial essay'. References also front cover, p3 + p4.
12007K3	**Films and Filming** July 1967 pp36 + 37. Photos + caption. p2. Full page advert.
12007K4	**Time and Tide** August 10-16 1967 p17 + 22. Brief references to film and Donald Pleasence.
12007K5	**Cinema X** Vol 1 No 12 pp16-19 n.d. 'Mrs 007 Talks About Her Latest Film. Mie Hana' (heroine of film). Photos. Ref. front cover also.
12007K6	**Mayfair** Vol 9 No 7 pp40-43. n.d. 'The Bird From You Only Live Twice, Ya Suko'. Photos by Michael Legge. Ref. front cover also.

A. FIRST EDITIONS

13007A1   Cr. 8vo p224 18s. 1 April 1965 Jonathan Cape. Black cloth, plain front cover, titled girl on spine 1st edn. Jacket Design by Richard Chopping, revolver, bullets and flies design front cover, extending to rear cover with title in black, spine not separately titled.*

13007A2   2nd impr. May 1965.

13007A3   3rd impr. June 1965. Dark grey cloth.

See 11007b3 **G.F. Sims (Rare Books)** Book Catalogue 62 Autumn 1965. Item 248 Uncorrected Proof Copy priced at £4.4.-.

Note: 1st edition also issued with white mottled wrappers (Lilly Library 143)

C. SOURCE MATERIAL, ETC.

13007C1   **Allen Dulles The Craft of Intelligence** Weidenfeld + Nicholson 2nd impr Aug 1964. Read by James Bond in Chapter 17 of The Man With the Golden Gun. (Without mentioning reference on p195 to greatest pleasure of author in reading of James Bond in On Her Majesty's Secret Service) (Bond Affair 18 Gant 136)

D. ANTHOLOGIES, ETC. – Serialisation

13007D1   **Playboy** April 1965 (U.S. edn.) pp64-70, 161-168. Part I. Illus. Howard Mueller.
p3 Reference to Fleming's preference for Playboy serialisation of this novel.
Also contains an article on food entitled 'From Russia With Love'.†

13007D2   **Playboy** May 1965 pp86-88, 165-174 Part II.

[13007D300 **Playboy** June 1965 Part III.]

13007D4   **Playboy** July 1965 pp88-90, 138-149 Conclusion.
Also p7 three letters re serialisation.
Also references on all issues front cover, p3 + p4, and on penultimate pages of April-June issues.

13007D5   Reader's Digest Condensed Book. The Reader's Digest Association. 1st edn. n.d. pp12-97. Illus by Roger Coleman. pp6-7 re the author. Patterned boards.

13007D6   De luxe edition of 13007D5, different binding, eps and title page.

E. BOOK REVIEWS

13007E1   **The Spectator** 2 April 1965 p447. Review by Simon Raven.

13007E2   **New York Times Book Review.** Section 7 22 August 1965 p15. Review by Anthony Boucher, also p8 – 9th on Best Seller List, p15 Full page advert, p16 Advert for **Gilt Edged Bonds** and **More Gilt Edged Bonds**

*See Note 3, p60.
†See Footnote, p23.

F. BOOK CLUB EDITION

13007F1   The Book Club n.d. (Jacket Design by Chrichard)

G. PAPERBACK EDITIONS (U.K.)

[13007G100 Pan Books Ltd. 1st edn 1966]

13007G2   2nd Printing 1967. Front Wrap of pistol + BOAC ticket.

13007G3   7th Printing 1968. Canadian price added to frontwrap and NZ price now in cents only.

13007G4   8th Printing 1969. Front wrap of pistol and coloured dancing girl.

13007G5   10th Printing 1972. Front Wrap of Cheese, pocket watch, etc.

H. FOREIGN EDITIONS

13007H1   New American Library New York n.d. Book Club edn. (1st U.S.A. edn. 23 Aug 1965)

13007H2   A Signet Book (NAL) First printing July 1966. Wraps.

13007H3   **L'Homme Au Pistolet D'Or.** Plon. Oct 1965. Wraps.

13007H4   **Altin Tabancali Adam.** Basak Yayinevi, Istanbul. 1966. Wraps.

J. FILM

13007J1   **Daily Express** 16 Dec 1974 p9 Serialisation of film. Day 1, also p1 ref + photo.

13007J2   **Daily Express** 17 Dec 1974 p13. Day 2.

13007J3   **Daily Express** 18 Dec 1974 p12. Day 3. Also p10 Review by Ian Christie.

13007J4   **Daily Express** 19 Dec 1974 p11. Day 4.

13007J5   **Daily Express** 20 Dec 1974 p11. End of Serial.

    Also James Bond Holiday in Thailand Competition in each issue.

K. FILM REVIEWS

13007K1   **Sunday Express** 7 July 1974 p19. Roderick Mann — 'What the New Bond Girl likes in her men' (Maud Adams). (pp19-20 only)

13007K2   **The Times** 20 December 1974 Newscutting: Review by David Robinson + photo.

    See also 13007J3 Daily Express 18 Dec 1974 p10. Review by Ian Christie.

A. FIRST EDITIONS

14007A1   Cr. 8vo p96. 1966 Jonathan Cape. Black cloth titled gilt on front cover and spine 1st edn. Jacket design by Richard Chopping with fish, shell and flies on front cover, titled in black on front cover and spine.

D. ANTHOLOGIES, PERIODICAL PUBLICATION, ETC.

14007D1   **The Sunday Times Colour Section** 4th February 1962 (The First Issue of this Section). p23 **The Living Daylights. A New James Bond Story by Ian Fleming** pp23-32.
Also Reference on front cover + p2.*

14007D2   **Argosy** June 1962 (U.S.A. Magazine for Men) pp22-4, 95-100. **Berlin Escape** by Ian Fleming (The Living Daylights). Illustrated by Lou Feck.

14007D3   **Playboy** March 1966 (U.S. edn.) pp60-62, 118-120. Illus Jeller. **Octopussy** (previously unpublished novelette according to front cover). (Defective copy, but text present)†

14007D4   **Playboy** April 1966 (U.S. edn) pp102-104, 170-176.

Also references on both issues on front cover, p3, p4 and on penultimate page of March issue.

E. BOOK REVIEW

14007E1   **The Spectator** 8 July 1966 p40 + 52. Review by Philip Larkin, also p51 advertisement for this book.

14007E2   **The Listener and BBC Television Review.** 14 July 1966 p65. Review by Anthony Burgess.

G. PAPERBACK EDITIONS (U.K.) (contains also **The Property of A Lady**)

[14007G100 Pan Books Ltd. 1st edn. 1966.]

14007G2   2nd printing 1968. Front wrap of butterfly, bullion bar and rocks. Rear wrap claims first appearance of **The Property of A Lady** in book form but see 15007A1.

14007G3   7th printing 1973. Front wrap of octopus, sniper's rifle and Sotheby's catalogue. No claim re **The Property of A Lady** on rear wrap.

H. FOREIGN EDITIONS

14007H1   New American Library. n.d. Book Club edition. (First U.S.A. edition 1966)

14007H2   A Signet Book (NAL). 1st printing July 1967. Wraps. (contains also **The Property of A Lady** and claims the first publication in book form)

*See Note 4, p60.
† See Note 5, p60.

A. FIRST EDITIONS

15007A1   **The Ivory Hammer: The Year at Sotheby's.** Longmans Green +
Co. Ltd. Illus. Cr. 4to p305 45s 11 November 1963 1st edn.
pp vii-xxi + plate **The Property of A Lady.** © Ian Fleming 1963.
This James Bond story concerning an auction at Sotheby's was
specially commissioned. (See Gant 166)*

C. SOURCE MATERIAL, ETC.

15007C1   The Times 21 November 1973 p20. Photo and article re Auction
of Faberge Imperial egg clock at Christies for £82,000, bought by
Kenneth Snowman (pp17-20 only)

D. PERIODICAL PUBLICATION

15007D1   **Playboy** January 1964. Tenth Anniversay Issue pp92-93, 200-
207. Illus.

Also references front cover, pp1-2 + 4. (Amis 114)

In a bound volume with original wraps containing issues for
January-June 1964.

May 1964 p16 Letter criticising A Property of A Lady.

April-June 1964 contains serialisation of You Only Live Twice.

(*See* 12007D1-4. June 1964 is a U.S. edn.)

BOOK REVIEWS, ETC.

See 15007D2 (Playboy May 1964 p16 Letter)

15007E1   **Sotheby Parke Bernet Publications 1977-78** Philip Wilson
Publishers Ltd. Wraps. p41. Reference to the first edition of a
James Bond short story in The Ivory Hammer 1962-1963.

G. PAPERBACK EDITIONS (U.K.)

See 14007G100, etc.

---

*(15007A1) The 'Kong' for 'King' error on p xiii of The Ivory Hammer is
corrected in the Playboy and paperback (14007G, H2) versions, which apart from
appropriate U.S. spelling variations all correspond. The omission of 'Road' after
Bayswater (p xxi) is not noted in any version.

A. FIRST EDITIONS

16007A1   Illus. Cr. 8vo p160. 12s6d. 29 November 1957 Jonathan Cape. Black cloth, plain front cover, titled in white on spine, 1st edn. Jacket Design by Denis Piper, red, grey and black with photograph of uncut diamonds, titled in black on front cover and spine. First book with © Glidrose Productions Ltd.

(Serialised in Sunday Times)

B. PROOF COPIES, INSCRIBED COPIES, ETC.

16007B1   2nd impr of 16007A1 November 1957 Signed 'Ian Fleming' on front endpaper.

E. BOOK REVIEWS

16007E1   **The Spectator** 13 December 1957. Review by Dan Jackson. p40 advertisement for book.

16007E2   **The New York Times Book Review.** 22 June 1958 p17. Review by John Barkham entitled 'Dark Deeds and Glittering Gems'.

16007E3   **John O'London's** 25 February 1960 p235. Review by Pat Wallace of the Great Pan Paperbacks of **The Diamond Smugglers, Dr No** and **Moonraker.**

G. PAPERBACK EDITIONS (U.K.)

[16007G100 Pan Books Ltd. Cr. 8vo p160 2s6d. 12 February 1960.]

16007G2   2nd Printing 1963. Front Wrap of two hands and a diamond. Price and Signature.

16007G3   6th Printing 1965. Front Wrap of two hands and a diamond. Different adverts at end (starting Thrilling Cities Part I)

16007G4   7th Printing 1965. Front Wrap of two hands and a diamond. Different adverts at end (start Thrilling Cities Parts I + II)

16007G5   7th Printing 1965. No price or signature on front wrap, overseas price on rear wrap. Different adverts at end (start Thrilling Cities Part I + II)

H. FOREIGN EDITIONS

[16007H100 Macmillan Co., New York, 160pp $3.50. June 1958. 1st U.S.A. edn.]

16007H2   Collier Books 1st Printing 1964 (U.S.A.)

A. FIRST EDITIONS

17007A1 Illus Roy 8vo p224 (+ erratum slip at p223) 1963 Jonathan Cape. Mottled grey boards with white cloth, spine titled gilt 1st edn. 30s. Jacket Design by Paul Davis, surrealist oil painting of Monte Carlo on front cover, titled in white and pink with pink spine titled in white. (Originally published in serial form in Sunday Times in 1959 and 1960, *See* 28007A3)

E. BOOK REVIEWS

17007E1 **The Listener** 14 November 1963 pp799-800. Review by Christopher Wordsworth

17007E2 **The Tatler + Bystander** 27th November 1963 p652. Brief review of Siriol Hugh-Jones.

Also p621-622. It's the Thought that Counts (article by J. Roger Baker on Christmas presents). 'Premium Bonds for Mr Ian Fleming because his own Bonds always win'.

17007E3 **The Spectator** 20th December 1963 pp827-8. Review by Dom Moraes.

17007E4 **Courier** Vol 42 No 4 April 1964. Review by Hugh Pierson (**You Only Live Twice** also reviewed)

(*See also* 24007A4 **The Spectator** 12 February 1960)

F. BOOK CLUB EDITION

17007F1 The Reprint Society Ltd. London. 1964. (Photo of Fleming on rear of d/w)

G. PAPERBACK EDITIONS

17007G1 Pan Books Ltd. p128 3s6d. 2 Oct 1964 1st edn. Part 1.

17007G2 Pan Books Ltd. 1965 1st edn. Part 2.

17007G3 3rd Printing 1965 Part 1. No price on cover.

17007G4 3rd Printing 1965 Part 1. Covers as 1st edn., internally as 17007G3 (adverts at end differ from 1st edn.)

H. FOREIGN EDITIONS

17007H1 A Signet Book (NAL) 3rd Printing n.d.

(First U.S.A. edition New American Library 1964)

A. FIRST EDITIONS

18007A1   **Adventure Number One** 9 x 6¼ p48 10s6d. 22 Oct 1964.
Jonathan Cape. White boards with picture of Chitty Chitty Bang
Bang diagonally across front cover extending to read cover, titled
in black 1st edn. Illus. by John Burningham. Dustwrapper similar
to covers.

18007A2   **Adventure Number Two** Jonathan Cape 1964 1st edn. Illus by
John Burningham. Similar cover and dustwrapper design.

18007A3   **Adventure Number Three** 9 x 6¼ p48 10s6d. 14 Jan 1965
Jonathan Cape 1st edn. Illus. by John Burningham. Similar cover
and dustwrapper design. (But Note 18007H1 below is dated 1964,
and thus predates this item).

18007a4   **The Complete Adventures of the Magical Car.** Jonathan Cape 1971.
1st omnibus edn. Illus by John Burningham.

18007a5   **Ian Fleming's Story of Chitty Chitty Bang Bang.** Adapted for
Beginning Readers by **Al Perkins.** Collins + Harvill 1st G.B. edn.
1969. Illus. by B. Tobey.

18007a6   **A Pop-Up Book. Chitty Chitty Bang Bang.** Based on the Ian
Fleming Story and abridged by **Albert G. Millar.** Random House,
New York, 1st edn. thus. 1968 (also sold thus in U.K.).
Designed by Paul Taylor. Illustrated by Gwen Gordon and Dave
Chambers.

E. BOOK REVIEWS

18007E1   Saturday Review. Children's Book Week Supplement. 7 November
1964 (U.S.A.) p53. Short Review.

18007E2X   The Junior Bookshelf February 1965. p32. (U.S.A.). Review.

18007E3X   The Horn Book Magazine April 1965. p167. (U.S.A.). Review by
Paul Heins.

F. BOOK CLUB EDITION

18007F1   Book Club Associates 1968. Illus by John Burningham.

G. PAPERBACK EDITION (U.K.)

18007G1   Pan Books Ltd. 8s6d. 26 July 1968 1st edn. Illus by John
Burningham.

H. FOREIGN EDITIONS

18007H1   Random House New York n.d. (1964) p114 $3.50. Illus. by John
Burningham (First U.S.A. edition).

18007H2   **Chitty Chitty Bang Bang La Voiture Merveilleuse.** Editions des
Deux Coqs d'Or Paris. 1969. Images de Glaite. Boards.

J. FILM

18007J1   **John Burke. Chitty Chitty Bang Bang. The Story of the Film.** Pan
Books Ltd. 1st edn 1968. (Pan Original)

18007J2   2nd Printing of 18007J1.

18007J3   Jigsaw Puzzle. 300 Pieces. **Chitty Chitty Bang Bang Cut Off By the Tide.** Tower Press (London) Ltd. 2114. In box, colour, scene from Albert R. Broccoli Film. © 1968 by Glidrose Productions Ltd and Warfield Productions Ltd. Box 7 x 9 x 1¼ ins (Companion puzzles: **Truly Scrumptious the Music Box Doll, Caractacus Potts tries Rocket Propulsion, Disaster with Potts Hair Cutting Machine).**

18007J4   Record, 45 r.p.m. E.M.I. Records Music for Pleasure No 1. **Chitty Chitty Bang Bang** and **Food, Glorious Food.**

K. FILM REVIEW

18007K1   **Kinematograph Weekly** 14 December 1968 p107. Photograph + details of films. (Lacks wraps)

This book was written by Fleming in December 1960, following a visit by Fleming to Kuwait as the guest of the Kuwait Oil Company, whose approval of the book was necessary before publication. Although Kuwait Oil Co. approved the book, the Kuwait Government objected to certain small parts concerning the adventurous past of Kuwait, and the book was therefore never published. The only bound copy is in the Lilly Library.

19007e1   **Sunday Express** 31 January 1971 p5. Article by Bernard Lee entitled '"Ban" on Fleming Book about Sheiks' with comments by Mrs Anne Fleming and John Pearson.

(*See* Pearson 325 + Lilly Library)

IN BOOK FORM

20007A1   **The Kemsley Manual of Journalism** p424. Illus. 9½ x 7½ Cassell
            + Co. Ltd. Nov. 1950 1st edn in d/w. pp238-246 Chapter by
            Fleming entitled 'Foreign News'. (This copy signed 'Kemsley' on
            title page) (Connolly 47)

20007A2   **Herbert O. Yardley. The Education of a Poker Player.** Jonathan
            Cape 1959 introduced by Ian Fleming pp7-9. (Fleming urged
            Cape to publish this American book in England) (Connolly 65)

20007G3   **Herbert O. Yardley. The Education of a Poker Player.** Introduc-
            tion by Ian Fleming. Sphere Books. Wraps. (First published in
            Great Britain in 1970 by Sphere Books on verso of title page,
            (but wraps quote English Newspaper reviews).)

20007A4   **Holiday Magazine Book of the World's Fine Food**: a treasury of
            adventures in gastronomy. Simon + Schuster New York 1960.
            1st Printing pp240-242 Article **London's Best Dining** by Ian
            Fleming 'A light-hearted lesson on how to get good English Food
            without bad English cooking'. (First published in **Holiday**).
            Fleming's name is not amongst the specially named contributors
            on the title page.

20007A5   **The Seven Deadly Sins.** William Morrow + Co. New York. **Special
            Foreword** by Ian Fleming (for U.S.A. edn. only) (© Sunday Times
            Publications Ltd 1962)

20007A6   **The Seven Deadly Sins.** Sunday Times Publications Ltd. 1962.
            Introduction by Raymond Mortimer. (U.K. edn. with no
            Fleming contribution)

20007A7   **Encore. The Sunday Times Book.** Michael Joseph 1962 1st edn.
            pp393-400 Article by Fleming entitled '**My Monte Carlo System**'
            (First published in The Sunday Times on 4th September 1960.)
            (Fleming's name as a contributor also appears on d/w.)

20007A8   **Encore. Second Year. The Sunday Times Book.** Michael Joseph
            1963 1st edn. pp367-371 Article by Fleming entitled '**A Golfing
            Nightmare**' (First published in the Sunday Times in 1957)

20007A9   **Hugh Edwards. All Night at Mr Stanyhurst's.** Introduced by Ian
            Fleming. Jonathan Cape 1963. Jacket design by Aedwyn Darroll,
            decorated by Eric Fraser. Introduction pp vii-xx.

20007a10   **Hugh Edwards. All Night at Mr Stanyhurst's.** Jonathan Cape
            1933 1st edn (1500 copies published)

20007a11   **Hugh Edwards. All Night at Mr Stanyhurst's.** The New Library.
            Jonathan Cape 1937 (3000 copies published)

20007G12   **Hugh Edwards. All Night at Mr Stanyhurst's.** Introduced by Ian
            Fleming. Pan Books Ltd. 1965. 1st edn. thus. Wraps.

20007A13   **Ian Fleming Introduces Jamaica** ed. **Morris Cargill**. Andre
            Deutsch. 1965. 1st edn. pp11-23 'Introducing Jamaica' by Ian
            Fleming. The majority of this introduction consists of Fleming's
            article in Horizon (21007A6) (Pearson 146-7). It also includes a
            reference to Fleming's recent meeting with Mr + Mrs James Bond
            (26007A17)

20007E14 **New Statesman** 8 October 1965 p531. Review by D.A.N. Jones
of **Ian Fleming Introduces Jamaica.**

20007A15 **Counterpoint** Compiled and Edited by **Roy Newquist.** George
Allen + Unwin Ltd. 1965 1st edn. pp209-216: Interview with Ian
Fleming in October 1963 (by Newquist) (Connolly 65)

20007A16 **Playboy Interview** selected by the editors of Playboy. Playboy
Press, Chicago, 1967 1st edn. pp14-29 **Ian Fleming,** with one page
introduction + photo, also brief reference. Preface p viii and photo
on front dustwrapper. (Interview first appeared in Playboy
December 1964 − 21007A19)

20007A17 **The Sunday Times Travel and Holiday Guide.** The Continent of
Europe. The Sunday Times, 1951. 1st edn. Leonard Russell and
Elizabeth Nicholas (editors) acknowledge 'the foreign news
service of Kemsley Newspapers . . . have helped us greatly'.
Almost certainly contains material by Fleming and at least
indirect source material for his books.

[20007A1800 Note: Fleming also wrote an electoral address for Charles
Morrison, the Conservative candidate for Devizes headed 'To
Westminster With Love'. May 1964 (Gant 144)]

IN PERIODICAL FORM

21007a1   **The Times** 18 March 1939 p12. (Centre page) **Article** by 'Our Diplomatic Correspondent' headed 'Trade Mission Mr Hudson Leaving To-day'.

21007A2   **The Times** 24 March 1939 p14. **Article** by 'Our Special Correspondent' headed 'Mr Hudson in Moscow − Meeting with M. Litvinoff − Situation in Europe Discussed'.

21007A3   **The Times** 25 March 1939 p12 (Centre page). **Article** by 'Our Special Correspondent' headed 'Soviet-British Talks − Mr Hudson sees Trade Chief − A Long Discussion'.

21007A4   **The Times** 25 March 1939 p11. **Article** by 'Our Special Correspondent' headed 'Moscow Trade Talks − The British Case Completed'.

21007A5   **The Times** 28 March 1939 p14 (Centre page). **Article** by 'Our Special Correspondent' headed 'Trade With Russia − Negotiations in London − Results of Moscow Talks'.

21007A6   **Horizon** December 1947 pp350-359. Article by Fleming '**Where Shall John Go XIII Jamaica** (Connolly 47)

21007A7X   **The Spectator** 18 August 1950 p211. Spectator Competition No 33 Set by Ian Fleming.

21007A8   **The Spectator** 15 September 1950 p291. **Report** by Ian Fleming on Spectator Competition No 33.

21007A9   **The Spectator** 5 August 1955 pp199-200. **Review** by Ian Fleming of Erskine Childers: The Riddle of the Sands (Ziegler 196)

21007E10   **The Spectator** 12 August 1955. Letters from W.P: Brooks Smith and G.M. Knocker re 'The Riddle of the Sands'.

21007A11   **The Spectator** 4 April 1958 pp424-5. **Automobilia** by Ian Fleming (Pearson 259, Ziegler 103), also contains p438 review of Dr No by Simon Raven.

21007E12   **The Spectator** 11 April 1958 p460. Letters from John Gloag and H.M. Malies re 21007A11 (Pearson 259 footnote)

21007A13   **The Spectator** 9 October 1959 pp466-7. **If I Were Prime Minister** by Ian Fleming.

21007E14   **The Spectator** 16 October 1959 p520. Letters from H. Maurice Palmer and G. Weedon 'Fleming for Premier'.

21007A15   **The London Magazine** December 1959 pp43-54. **Raymond Chandler** by Ian Fleming.

21007A16   **The Bookman** November 1960 p21. **Review** by Fleming of 'The Pass Beyond Kashmir' by Berkeley Mather entitled 'Adventure in the Haggard-Buchan School'.

21007A17   **The Spectator** 26 October 1962 p636. **Letter** from Ian Fleming entitled '**Bondage**' concerning the publication of 3 separate items relating to him in the previous week's Spectator.

21007A18 **The Sunday Times Colour Section** 18th November 1962 pp18-22.
Article by Fleming entitled **'James Bond's Hardware'**. Illus.
Reference on front cover. (*See also* 32007A600)

21007A19 **Playboy** December 1964 pp97-106 (+ photo) Playboy Interview:
Ian Fleming. Reference on front cover and on p3 where it is
stated to be Fleming's last interview. (*See* 20007A16)

21007a20 Untraced book review by Fleming. **James Clavell. King Rat.** A
Panther Book 5th reprint May 1966 Wraps. 1st published Michael
Joseph 1963. 'Terrifyingly Exciting' Ian Fleming — according to
front wrap.

See also 20007A4 **Holiday.**

22007A1   **Typescript Memorandum** dated 8th July 1948 from Ian Fleming
as Foreign Manager Kemsley Newspapers to Lord Kemsley
(Chairman), initialled by Fleming in biro and by Kemsley in
pencil.

22007A2   **Agreement** (Blank folded 4pp legal form) (1948) between
'Kemsley Newspapers Ltd and . . . Signatory Ian Fleming, Foreign
Manager'.

22007A3   **Naked Hollywood.** Photos by **Weegee**, written by **Mel Harris.**
Pellegrini + Cudahy New York 1953 1st edn. **Inscribed** on front
end paper 'Dilys + Leonard Alas – only for the record Ian'.
Dilys Powell and Leonard Russell, like Fleming, were employed
by the Sunday Times, as also was Ernestine Carter, from the
collection of whose husband, John Carter, an Etonian contemporary and friend of Fleming, this book was bought. (With t.l.s.
dated 1st May 1976 by Dilys Russell stating that she and her
husband knew Fleming well, but that they had sold their inscribed
copies of his books some time ago) (*See also* 28007A7)

22007A4   **The Book Collector.** Vol 1 No 1 Spring 1952. The Queen Anne
Press Ltd. p xiii shows editorial board as Ian Fleming, John
Hayward + P.H. Muir.

22007A5   **G.F. Sims Catalogue** 64 (c1966). Item 108: Eight Ian Fleming
first editions inscribed to William Plomer £150.

22007A6   **Peter Fleming. The Sixth Column.** A Singular Tale of Our Times
Rupert Hart-Davis 1951. Dedicated 'To My Brother Ian'.
(Described by author as a 'non-thrilling thriller'.)

22007A7   **Alaric Jacob. Scenes from a Bourgeois Life.** Secker + Warburg
1949. 1st edn. Fleming was put into this book under the
pseudonym of Hugo Dropmore (Pearson 73)

22007A8   **W. Somerset Maugham. Ten Novels and Their Authors.**
Heinemann 1947 1st edn. Maugham wrote to Fleming whilst he
was writing this book, which resulted in Fleming successfully
negotiating with Maugham for the prepublication serial rights for
the Sunday Times. (Pearson 242-245)

22007A9   **Charles Graves. None but the Rich.** The Life and Times of the
Greek Syndicate. Cassell + Co. Ltd. 1963. 1st edn. Zographos and
the Greek Syndicate provided Fleming with much of the background for **Casino Royale**; and Fleming began a short story not
long before his death in which Bond meets Zographos – possibly
inspired by this book (Pearson 193-4)

22007A10 **Autograph of Phyllis Bottome** (novelist 1884-1963) A strong
influence on Fleming's early life (Pearson 33-43)

22007A11 **Life and Letters** Vol VII No 38 July 1931 pp26-45. 'Under the
Bandstand' by Peter Fleming. First published fictional account of
violence by Ian or Peter Fleming.

22007A12 **Exhibition of Books 1951.** Festival of Britain. Arranged by the National Book League at the Victoria and Albert Museum. Catalogue. p9. Ian Fleming amongst list of lenders (refers to items 224 + 242 in The Scientist Section — P.H. Muir was on the advisory panel of this section and Peter Fleming on that of another section).

22007A13 **Printing and the Mind of Man.** Catalogue of the Exhibitions at The British Museum and at Earls Court, London 15-27 July 1963. Organized in connexion with the eleventh International Printing Machinery and Allied Trades Exhibition. F.W. Bridges + Son Ltd and the Association of British Manufacturers of Printers Machinery (Proprietary) Ltd. 1963 Wraps. 44 of the exhibits were lent from the Ian Fleming collection, a number exceeded only by Kings College, Cambridge (51).

22007A14 **The Ian Fleming Collection of 19th-20th Century Source Material Concerning Western Civilization Together with Originals of the James Bond — 007 Tales.** Foreword by David A. Randall and Percy Muir. Lilly Library Publication No XII Indiana University Office of Publications. Limited to 1500 copies. Wraps. n.d. (1970) (Indiana University bought from Fleming's executors the typescripts of all his works except **The Man With The Golden Gun** and Fleming's own copies of his novels).

22007A15 Three nineteenth century heraldic bookplates of persons with the name of Fleming showing the crest and motto which appear as endpapers in Pearson and front wrap in Lilly Library.

22007A16 Theatre Poster. **Hay Fever** by **Noel Coward.** Duke of York's Theatre. 12½ x 20 ins. Fleming hero-worshipped Coward (who was a godparent of Fleming's son Caspar). (Pearson 115, 212). This production of Hay Fever starred Celia Johnson (Fleming's sister in law) with a smaller role for Lucy Fleming (Fleming's niece).

22007A17 **Lone Star James Bond 007 Super Action Set.** Lone Star Productions Ltd., Welham Green, Herts. Cat No 1210. © Eon Productions Ltd/Glidrose Pub Ltd. 1973 (but still on sale in 1978). Consists of gun with silencer, shoulder holster, 007 badge, Walkie Talkie Set, 2 hand grenades, decoder.

23007A1   **B.D. Mascott. 003½ The Adventures of James Bond Junior.** Illus. Christopher Chamberlain. Jonathan Cape 1967 1st edn. Copyright by Glidrose Productions Ltd.

23007A2   **Robert Markham** (pseud. Kingsley Amis) **Colonel Sun** A James Bond Adventure. p256 21s. 28 March 1968. Jonathan Cape. Jacket painting by Tom Adams.

23007C3   **Observer** 31 March 1968. Colour Magazine pp10-13. 'The New James Bond Kingsley Amis (alias Robert Markham) Explains' — concerns background to writing of **Colonel Sun.** (Tom Adams dustwrapper as colour spread illustration)

23007D4   **Daily Express** 30 May 1970 p12. Strip Cartoon: James Bond by Ian Fleming. Drawing by Horak 1327 (**Colonel Sun**). Also on p2 Article headed 'I'm no spy, says Colonel' with references to the fact that he is not quite like James Bond.

23007D5   **Daily Express** 5 August 1970 p9. Strip Cartoon 1380 Horak (**Colonel Sun**)

23007D6   **Daily Express** 7 March 1968 p14. Strip Cartoon 670 Horak (pp13-14 only)

23007D7   **Daily Express** 11 Feb 1971 p12. Strip Cartoon 1541 Horak.

23007D8   **Daily Express** 14 Oct 1971 p21. Strip Cartoon 1748 Horak.

23007D9   **Daily Express** 18 May 1972 p17. Strip Cartoon 1931 Horak.

23007a10   **The Bookseller** 30 December 1967. Advertisement in colour, front and rear covers of d/w by Tom Adams for **Colonel Sun** to be published 4th April 1968.

23007E11   **The Listener** 28 March 1968 p11. Review by D.J. Enright of **Colonel Sun.**

23007E12   **Newsweek** 6 May 1968 (U.S.A.) pp108 + 111. Review by Paul D. Zimmerman of **Colonel Sun.**

23007F13   **Robert Markham. Colonel Sun.** The Companion Book Club. n.d.

23007F14   **The Companion** No 205. (Folded leaflet of The Companion Book Club). Synopsis of **Colonel Sun** illus with biography of Kingsley Amis.

23007G15   **Robert Markham. Colonel Sun.** Pan Books Ltd 1970 1st thus. Wraps.

23007G16   **Robert Markham. Colonel Sun.** Pan Books Ltd 1974 8th Printing. Different Pan device on Backstrip and different prices.

23007G17   **Robert Markham. Colonel Sun.** Triad/Panther Books 1977 1st thus. Wraps.

[23007H1800 **Robert Markham. Colonel Sun.** Harper + Row $5.95. 1968.]

23007A19   **The James Bond 007 Annual.** World Distributors (Manchester) Ltd. Copyright Eon Productions Ltd + Glidrose Productions Ltd 1966. (Most of the photographic illustrations relate to the film of **Thunderball,** the remainder of the book concerns spies — mainly fiction)

23007A20 **The James Bond Annual.** World Distributors (Manchester) 1968. Copyright Eon Productions Ltd + Glidrose Productions Ltd. Also strip cartoon story of **Live and Let Die** reproduced by arrangement with Daily Express.

23007A21 Another variant copy of 23007A20 with colours of illustrations pp80-93 transposed.

23007A22 **John Pearson. James Bond – The Authorized Biography of 007.** A Fictional Biography. Sidgwick + Jackson 1973 1st edn.

23007D23 **Sunday Telegraph** 2, 9, 16 + 23 September 1973 pp6-7 each issue. **Is James Bond Real . . . and Alive? John Pearson's Authorised Biography of 007.** Drawings by Klim Forster. (Prepublication serialisation). Also p11 Issue 16 September 1973. Letter from M.B. Clemens stating that Kipling was the first author to put 007 into a book in a short story about a railway locomotive 007, published in 1898.

23007A24 **Christopher Wood. James Bond, The Spy Who Loved Me.** The Book of the Film. Triad/Panther Books. 1977 1st thus. (First published by Jonathan Cape 1977)

23007E25 **New Statesman** 1 July 1977 pp25-26. Kingsley Amis review of 'James Bond the Spy Who Loved Me' entitled 'Shaken, But Not Stirred'. 'Always sensitive to criticism couched in moral terms, Fleming stipulated that this story of his should never be filmed; the title alone might be used'.

24007A1 **The Spectator** 23 December 1955 pp862-3. **His Word His Bond by IXN FLXMXNG.**

24007A2 **Spectrum — A Spectator Anthology.** ed. **Ian Gilmour and Iain Hamilton.** Longmans Green + Co. 1956 1st edn. pp80-81. **His Word, His Bond.** Ixn Flxmxng Short parody 'rescued from a wastepaper basket by Mr John Russell' Chapter XIX 'YMCA again'.

24007A3 **Punch** 13 November 1957 pp567-8. Alex Atkinson. **Scersh.** (With all due respect to Commander Ian Fleming)

24007A4 **The Spectator** 12 February 1960 p207. **Thrilling Cities; 32781 Queen of the North West by I–N FL–M––G (Creator of J–––s B––d) Bernard Levin.**

[24007A500 **The Harvard Lampoon 1962. Alligator by I*n Fl*m*ng.** (Amis 63-4)]

24007A6 **The London Magazine** April 1963 pp8-23. **Bond Strikes Camp an extravaganza by Cyril Connolly** (Amis 64)

[24007A700 **The Auk** 1964. Avian Flemish. **On Her Majesty's Ornithological Service,** reprinted in **Mrs James Bond: How 007 Got His Name (26007A17)]**

24007A8 **Eton Microcosm** ed. Anthony Cheetham + Derek Parfit. Sidgwick + Jackson 1964 1st edn. Illus. Edward Pagram. pp121-2 Whodunit competition: parody of James Bond.

24007A9 **Punch** 9 March 1966 p336. 'The Men from S.P.Y.' Cartoon of James Bond in drag with caption 'British Intelligence won't forget this sacrifice, James Bond'.

24007A10 **Men's Digest** No 67 June 1966 (U.S.A.) pp16-19. 'Vintage-Bond: Italian-style with Isobella' (Borgonelli, who is to star in new Italian take-off film on the 007 craze entitled 'James Bond Spoof Girl').

24007A11 **Playboy** July and August 1966. Parts I + II **Sol Weinstein: On the Secret Service of Her Majesty the Queen.** Parody 'further adventures, already, of secret agent Oy Oy 7, Israel Bond'. July 1966 Part I pp56-62, 66, 125-138, also reference on front cover and details of other adventures p3: August 1966 Part II pp76-78, 96, 158-178, also reference on front cover + p3.
Also July 1966 pp75-79 'Sean Connery Strikes Again' — article on Warner Bros farce 'A Fine Madness' and pp102-109 'Ursula' — article on Ursula Andress with references to film of Dr No

24007A12 **Pl*yb*y.** Harvard Lampoon Parody of Playboy Vol 1 No 1 1966 pp70-75, 80-88, 94-96, 100-101. **Toadstool — J*m*s B*nd Thriller I*n Fl*m*ng,** a complete novelette. Reference on p3 to this being 'his first novel since his death' (Gant 128)

24007a13 **Playboy** December 1966 p20. Editorial reply to reader's letter asking about authenticity of Pl*yb*y. ('most ambitious of a long line of collegiate parodies of Playboy that have been produced with our permission')

24007A14 **James Blonde. Secret Agent 006.95 (marked down from 007.00)**
'**The Man from T.A.N.T.E.**' with **DR NO? + GOLDFLAKER.**
Starring **Marty Bell + Larry Foster.** Colpix Records CPL-495
U.S.A. 1965 ($33\frac{1}{3}$ r.p.m. Record)

24007A15 **The Big Ben Bunkside Book** or For Home the Bell Tolls compiled
by **Jocelyn Piper Whittingstall.** Lewis Frewin 1966 1st edn:
unnumbered pages; contains photograph of Lord Hailsham stand-
ing in the sea in bathing mask + snorkel with caption 'Look down,
Look up, Look out — here comes Bond!'

24007A16 **Private Eye** 14 April 1967. Front Cover portrait of Harold Wilson
headlined 'This Man is James Bond' and small inset photo of de
Gaulle entitled 'Doctor NON'.

24007E17 **Book Collecting and Library Monthly** January 1969 p282 article
Bond Strikes Camp referring to Cyril Connolly's satire on James
Bond, limited to 50 copies and the rarest of Connolly's books.
(*See* 24007A6)

24007A18 **The Life and Times of Private Eye 1961-1971** Edited by **Richard
Ingrams.** Penguin Books 1971. 1st edn. p56. **Aesop Revisited. The
Snob's Dick Barton.** (Comic strip life of Ian Phlegm and his
adventures of Basildon Bond)

24007A19 **Daily Express** 4 November 1974 p1 Headline 'Pay Cut for James
Bond'. (Article on the effect of new Defence cuts on the Secret
Service.)

24007A20 **TV Times** 5-11 Nov 1977 Granada edition p93. From Mother
With Love . . . 007's pie thriller. (Recipe for steak and kidney pie
by Kathie Webber. 'But his favourite was his Mum's steak and
kidney pie'. [Roger Moore])

24007H21 **Wallace MacKentzy. Allan Beebe Sfida Agente 007** (Everybody
in the Dark Without Glasses). Tre Cerchi, Roma, 1962. Wraps.

24007H22 **Bill Wharton. The Real 007.** Pyramid Books New York 1st
Printing July 1969. Wraps: 'The Fantastically True Escapades of
Langridge — the superspy'. He was the living model for Ian
Fleming's James Bond'.

24007H23 **Rod Gray. To Russia with L.U.S.T.** Undercover Agent Oh Oh **Sex**
tries to penetrate Russia and vice versa. A Tower Book, New
York. n.d. (Mildly pornographic sexual exploits of a woman spy.)

24007H24 **Ray Galton and Alan Simpson. The Spy With a Cold Nose.** Arrow
Books Original. 1st edn July 1967. Wraps. With illustrations from
the film of this story. (Humorous spy story with Fleming
references including a chapter entitled 'Dr Yes'.)

24007H25 **George Mikes. The Spy Who Died of Boredom.** Quartet Books
Ltd. 1974 1st thus. Wraps. (Humorous novel concerning Russian
spy who reads James Bond stories.)

24007H26 Royal West of England Academy Annual Exhibition Catalogue
November 1976 p55 refers to Ian Fleming R.S.A., R.S.W.,
R.W.A. of Aberdeen.

(Books where the publishers quote a critic
comparing the book to Fleming)

25007A1   **Arthur Tietjen. Soviet Spy Ring.** Pan Special 1961 1st edn. (about
Lonsdale, Kroger, etc.) 'As fantastic and exciting as any James
Bond thriller'. (A prominent character is Det-Superintendent
'Moonraker' Smith of Special Branch).

25007A2   **Len Deighton. Funeral in Berlin.** Jonathan Cape 1964 1st edn.
'James Bond's most serious rival – to be filmed by Harry
Salzman, producer of Dr No and From Russia With Love'. (D/W)

25007A3   **John Gardner. The Liquidator.** Corgi Books 5th reprint 1967.
Wraps (1st pub 1964). Introductory blurb full of comparisons of
Fleming/Bond and Gardner/Boysie Oakes.

25007A4   **Adam Diment. The Dolly Dolly Spy.** Pan Books Ltd. 1967 1st
thus. Wraps. (Three of the reviews quoted refer to Fleming or
Bond in comparison).

25007A5   **Adam Diment. The Great Spy Race.** Pan Books Ltd. 1969 1st
thus. Wraps. '. . . and goings on that make James Bond look like
Gary Cooper'.

25007A6   **Ronald Kirkbride. The Short Night.** Pan Books Ltd. 1971 1st
thus. Wraps. (1st Pub. 1968). Two reviews state 'Kirkbride is to
be rated above Fleming'.

25007A7   **James Mayo. Asking For It.** Pan Books Ltd. 1972 1st thus.
'James Bond's successor as Secret Service sexual athlete'. Adverts.
at end mention other books by Mayo: Shamelady: 'I think Ian
Fleming would have approved' and The Man Above Suspicion:
'nearest thing to Bond that's left'.

25007A8   **Frederick Forsyth. The Day of the Jackal.** Corgi Books. 3rd
reprint. 1973. Wraps. (1st Pub. 1971). 'Easily beating Ian
Fleming on his own ground'.

25007A9   **T.A. Waters. Love That Spy.** Lancer Books Inc. New York 1968.
'Patrick was used to sex. Neither James Bond nor Steve Victor
had anything on him in that department'.

26007A1 **William Plomer. Ian Fleming 28th May 1908-12th August 1964.** Address given at the Memorial Service. Privately Printed. Wraps.

26007A2 Another copy of 26007A1 bound in buckram slip case. (Goldfinger was dedicated to 'William Plomer, my gentle reader'.) *See also* 27007A4 and 22007A5.

26007A3 **Henry A. Ziegler. Ian Fleming, The Spy Who Came in With the Gold.** Duell Sloan and Pearce, New York 1965 1st edn. d/w.

26007A4 **Richard Gant. Ian Fleming: The Man With the Golden Pen.** A life by Richard Gant. Mayflower-Dell Paperback. April 1966. 1st reprint (1st pub April 1966). Wraps. 'The first full life', but *see* 26007A3 above.

26007A5 **John Pearson. The Life of Ian Fleming.** Jonathan Cape 1966. 1st edn. d/w.

26007A6 Another copy of 26007A5, but published defective and incomplete. (Paper of pp161-2 incomplete and lacks pp175-178.)

26007D7 **Reader's Digest August 1968** pp146-170. **John Pearson.** James Bond's Last Victim in Two-Book Supplement, condensed from **'The Life of Ian Fleming'.** Reference also on front cover.

26007E8 **London Magazine** Vol 6 No 7 October 1966. Review by Alan Ross of **John Pearson's The Life of Ian Fleming.**

26007E9 **New Statesman** 28 October 1966 p628. Review by V.S. Naipaul of **John Pearson's Life of Ian Fleming.** Reference also on front page (609).

26007E10 **The Spectator** 28 October 1966 pp552-3. Book Review/article by Simon Raven entitled 'The Natural Man' re **The Life of Ian Fleming** by **John Pearson.**

26007E11 **Cyril Connolly. The Evening Colonnade.** David Bruce + Watson 1973 1st edn. d/w. (Series of Essays) pp388-391 on reading **John Pearson's** biography (1966).

26007F12 **John Pearson. The Life of Ian Fleming.** The Companion Book Club. n.d. d/w.

26007F13 De luxe edition of 26007F12. n.d. d/w.

26007G14 **John Pearson. The Life of Ian Fleming.** Creator of James Bond. Pan Books Ltd. 1967 1st edn thus. Wraps.

26007E15 **The New York Times Book Review** Section 7. 11 December 1966 pp34 + 36. Review by Albert Goldman of 26007A5 entitled 'The Elegant Narcissist'.

[26007H1600 **John Pearson. The Life of Ian Fleming.** McGraw-Hill Book Company. New York 338pp. $6.95]

26007A17 **Mrs James Bond** (Mary Wickham Bond). **How 007 Got His Name.** Collins 1966 1st edn. d/w. (*See* 34007A3)

26007A18 **Ivar Bryce. You Only Live Once.** Memories of Ian Fleming. Weidenfeld + Nicholson 1975 1st edn. d/w. Bryce's surname was appropriated by Fleming in **Live and Let Die** (Pearson 280).

27007A1   **Life International** 24 September 1962 pp83-86. Tim Green. 'The Master of Agent 007'. Photo illus.

27007A2   **Time.** 21 August 1964 Atlantic Edition. pp18-19. 'The Man With the Golden Bond'. Obituary Notice + photo.

27007A3   **British Books** September 1964 p11. Obituary of Ian Fleming.

27007A4   **Encounter** January 1965 pp64-66. 'William Plomer: Ian Fleming Remembered' (*See* 26007A1 also).

27007A5   **The Book Collector** Winter 1964 pp431-3. Commentary. Editorial obituary notice of Ian Fleming.

27007A6   **The Book Collector** Spring 1965 pp24-33. P.H. Muir. Ian Fleming: A Personal Memoir. (1964 Index tipped in.)

27007a7   **Bibliography in Britain 3** 1964 Oxford Bibliographical Society. 1965. Item 368. p27 refers to 27007A5.

27007a8   **Bibliography in Britain 4** 1965 Oxford Bibliographical Society. 1967. Item 380, p30 refers to 27007A6.

28007A1   **Peter Fleming. One's Company.** Jonathan Cape 1934. 1st edn. References to brother Ian pp27, 28, 66.

28007A2   **Percy Muir. Minding My Own Business.** An Autobiography. Chatto + Windus. 1956 1st edn. d/w. References pp187, 190, 196, 204-5, 217-8. Fleming and Muir were both directors of Elkin Mathews and editors of The Book Collector (*See also* 22007A4, 27007A5 and 27007A6)

28007A3   **The Sunday Times.** A Pictorial Biography of One of the World's Great Newspapers. February 1961 (Compliments slip of Roy Thomson tipped in). Photograph of board and Ian Fleming on first page (Planning the Paper). Photograph of Fleming and serialisation of 'The Thrilling Cities' on page relating to serials.

28007A4   **H. Montgomery Hyde. The Quiet Canadian.** The Secret Service Story of Sir William Stephenson. Hamish Hamilton 1962 1st edn. d/w. References pp18, 238, 241 (also reference to Ivar Bryce (26007A18) p181)

28007A5   **Michael S. Howard. Jonathan Cape, Publisher.** Herbert Jonathan Cape, G. Wren Howard. Jonathan Cape 1971 1st edn. Many references.

28007a6   **The Times** 17 December 1974. Newspaper cutting of obituary notice of Michael S. Howard, which refers to Fleming.

28007A7   **Harold Hobson, Philip Knightley, Leonard Russell. The Pearl of Days.** An intimate Memoir of the Sunday Times 1822-1972. Hamish Hamilton 1972 1st edn. d/w. Many references (all except one in chapters written by Leonard Russell) + 2 illus. (*See also* 22007A3)

28007A8   **Duff Hart-Davis. Peter Fleming. A Biography.** Jonathan Cape 1974. 1st edn. d/w. Many references + photo illus.

28007A9   **Obituaries from The Times** (1961-1970). Advertising leaflet 6pp. January 1976. With quotation from Ian Fleming obituary.

28007A10   **Now + Then** No 106. Autumn 1960. p21 Full page photo of Fleming and caption reference to forthcoming publication of **Thunderball** in March 1961.

28007A11   **Punch** 18 July 1962. Ronald Searle. Caricature: 'Searle's-eye View of Ian Fleming' + photo.

28007A12X **Who Was Who** 1961-1970 p382 Entry re Ian Fleming.

> *See also* 1007D3 **Gilt Edged Bonds** pp v-xxi
>   2007D1 **Best Secret Service Stories** pp13-16
>   3007D1 **Best Gambling Stories** p10
>   4007J1 **James Bond, Diamonds Are Forever** Film Brochure
>   8007D5 **Best Secret Service Stories 2** pp9-18.

29007A1   **O.E.A.** List of Members May 1st 1940 1440-1940 Founders Day.
           Privately Printed for members of the Old Etonian Association 1940.
           Wraps. (Cover design by Reynolds Stone, an Etonian contem-
           porary of Fleming). Fleming entry at foot of p88.

29007A2   **Alaric Jacob. A Window in Moscow.** Collins 1946 1st edn. p264
           brief reference to meeting Fleming in Cairo in late 1944. (*See also*
           22007A7)

29007A3   **Eton Ramblers 1953 Active List** (of Cricketers). 1953. Wraps.
           120pp. p32 entry I.L. Fleming, 8, Crosby Square, London E.C.3.

29007A4   **Peter Fleming. The Gower Street Poltergeist.** Rupert Hart-Davis.
           1958. 1st edn. p157 reference to Ian Fleming becoming Victor
           Ludorum at Eton.

29007A5   **Punch** 20 February 1963 p259. Design for a Cabinet, Labour
           Looks Ahead. 'Mr Ian Fleming is earmarked for the War Office'.

29007A6   **S.P.B. Mais and Gillian Mais. Caribbean Holiday.** Alvin Redman
           1963. 1st edn. d/w. pp91-2 brief references to Goldeneye +
           Fleming.

29007A7   **Allen Dulles. The Craft of Intelligence.** Weidenfeld + Nicolson.
           2nd impr. August 1964. p195 brief reference to Ian Fleming +
           James Bond. (*See* 30007A16)

29007A8   **Russell Braddon. Roy Thomson of Fleet Street.** Collins 1965 1st
           edn. d/w. p276.

29007A9   **Len Deighton's London Dossier.** Penguin Books 1967 1st edn.
           Wraps. p107 (chapter by Godfrey Smith on Self-indulgence)
           'I once peered through the curtains on a dark night and saw Ian
           Fleming entertaining a mysterious lady to dinner'. (re Washington
           Hotel, W.1.)

29007A10   **The Sunday Times Magazine** 23 November 1969 p69 brief
           reference to 6 votes from readers for Ian Fleming as '1001st
           Maker of the Twentieth Century'. (Neil Armstrong received most
           votes, followed by Jim Clark + Yehudi Menuhin)

29007A11   **The Times** 27 December 1973 p2. Article on the drowning of
           three men in the Hull Trawler Ian Fleming which sank after
           running into a cliff in a fjord in Northern Norway.

29007A12   **Sunday Express** 3 February 1974 p2. Town Talk (gossip) column
           headed 'Ian Fleming's son Caspar leaves Oxford – It wasn't the
           life for me'.

29007A13   **The Sunday Times Magazine** 5 January 1975 pp31, 32. Brief
           references to Fleming in an article on Eric Ambler entitled 'The
           Ambler Lily'.

29007A14   **The Times** 4 October 1975 p3. Article headed 'Ian Fleming's son
           found dead at home' (pp3-4 only)

29007A15   **The Times** 6 October 1975 p22. Death Notice re Caspar Fleming
           (pp1-2, 21-2 only)

29007A16 **The Times** 14 October 1975 p3. Article headed 'Son of Ian Fleming took own life' re inquest on death of Caspar Fleming on 2nd October (pp3-4 only)

29007A17 **Daily Express** 14 October 1975 p3. Short article headed 'Author's son killed himself' (pp3-4 only)

29007A18 **The Times** 7 January 1976. Newscutting re death of Major David Fleming, an insurance broker and a nephew of Ian Fleming, while setting fire to his own stable block.

29007A19 **Investors Chronicle** 13 August 1976 pp460-461. Article 'Fashion catches up with Robert Fleming' (merchant bankers) – brief references to Ian Fleming and Peter Fleming p461 (pp459-461 only)

29007A20 **The Times** 4 November 1976 p11. Article by Sheridan Morley on Diane Cilento in which she says that Ian Fleming suggested to her that she should write, whilst on Bond film location, and the result was her first novel. (pp11 + 12 only)*

29007A21 **The Sunday Times Magazine** 23 January 1977 p13. Reference to Ian Fleming and photograph from **Dr No** film in review of first 25 years of Queen's reign.

29007A22 **The Guardian** 3 March 1977. Photograph and article re Colt Python .357 presented to Fleming by Colt Company sold (apparently unused) at Christies for £990. (newscutting only)

See also 1007D1 **The Spy's Bedside Book** p12
8007D2 **To Catch a Spy** pp18 + 22
17007E2 The Tatler + Bystander 27 Nov 1963.

---

*The Manipulator (1967), suitably about a film festival and dedicated 'For Sean'. Cigarette smoke is exhaled in Chapter 7 (cf Pearson 205).

30007A1   O.F. Snelling. **Double 0 Seven James Bond.** A Report. Neville Spearman. Holland Press. 1964. 1st edition. (Bond Affair 152)

30007E2   **The Spectator** 2 October 1964 pp444-5. Review by Simon Raven of **Double 0 Seven James Bond.**

30007G3   O.F. Snelling. **007 James Bond A Report.** A Panther Book 2nd reprint June 1965 Wraps. (1st Panther edition Jan 1965). Contains a special preface referring to Fleming's death, not in the Neville Spearman edition.

30007H4   O.F. Snelling. **007 James Bond A Report.** A Signet Book (NAL) 1st Printing April 1965. Wraps.

30007A5   Kingsley Amis. **James Bond Dossier.** Jonathan Cape 1965 1st edition. Jacket design by Jan Pienkowski based on Richard Chopping designs. (Inscription on front end paper 'to 008 from 006'.) (Bond Affair 154)

30007B6   Kingsley Amis. **James Bond Dossier.** Jonathan Cape. Proof copy in wraps and proof dustwrapper. (Provisional publication date 27 May).

30007d7   **The Spectator** 7 May 1965 p605. Advertisement re the forth-coming serialisation of **The James Bond Dossier** in the Sunday Mirror.

30007E8   **The Spectator** 28 May 1965 pp694-5. Review by Simon Raven of **The James Bond Dossier** entitled 'Amis and the Eggheads'.

30007e9   **The Spectator** 11 June 1965 p753. Letter from Michael Scott: Amis and the Eggheads.

30007E10   **London Magazine** June 1965 pp92-6. Review of **The James Bond Dossier** by Gavin Ewart entitled Bondage.

30007G11   Kingsley Amis. **The James Bond Dossier.** Pan Books Ltd. 1966. 1st edn.

30007H12   Kingsley Amis. **The James Bond Dossier.** New American Library. Printed on dustwrapper 'Is he in Hell or is he in Heaven − That damned elusive 007?'

30007E13   **The New York Times Book Review** Section 7 25 July 1965 p4. Review by Al Hine of **The James Bond Dossier** with photograph from film of **Dr No.**

30007A14   Lt-Col William ('Bill') Tanner. **The Book of Bond or Every Man His Own 007.** Jonathan Cape Ltd. 1st edn. 1965.

30007G15   Lt-Col William ('Bill') Tanner. **The Book of Bond.** Pan Books Ltd. 1st Printing 1966.

30007A16   **For Bond Lovers Only.** Compiled and Edited by **Sheldon Lane.** Panther Books Ltd. 1st edn. August 1965. Wraps. (One girl on front wrap). Contains
007 and Me Ian Fleming presented by Jack Fishman
The Blood Guts and Girls Man Sean Connery
Room 39 by Donald McLachlan
The Man from the Ipcress File (Len Deighton) by Peter Evans
The 007 Armoury by Jack Thomas

Bonds Broads (Anon)
007 and Friends (Photographs from films, etc.)
The Thriller Business. A Verbal Exchange between Fleming and
    Simenon by Frederick Sands
Talking about Spies with Ian Fleming by J. Bernard Hutton
    (*See* 34007A4)
Iced Water and Cool Customers by Raymond Chandler
The Man who's got 007's Number by Henry Gris + Sheldon Lane
The Spy Boss who Loves Bond by Allen Dulles (*See* 29007A7)

30007A17 **For Bond Lovers Only.** Panther Books Ltd. 1st reprint June 1966
    (Two girls on front wrap)

30007A18 **The Bond Affair.** Edited by **Oreste del Buono + Umberto Eco.**
    Macdonald. 1st English edition 1966 (First published in Italy in
    1965 as Il Caso Bond by Casa Ed. Valentino Bompiani.)
    Translated by R.A. Downie.
    A Popular Phenomenon by Lietta Tornabuoni
    The Narrative Structure in Fleming by Umberto Eco
    Myths and History in the Epic of James Bond by Romano Calisi
    Bond's Women by Furio Colombo
    The Psychoanalysis of 007 by Fausto Antonini
    Technology in the World of James Bond by G.B. Zorzoli
    The Credible and the Incredible in the Films of 007 by Andrea
        Barbato
    James Bond and Criticism by Laura Lilli
    James Bond and Criticism: Sources and References.
    (Rear dustwrapper advertises Orient Express by Michael Barsley
    (5007C3) with references to Fleming and Bond.)

[30007A1900 **L.M. Starkey. James Bond: His World of Values.** Lutterworth
    Press. 70pp. 1966.]

30007A20 **Ann S. Boyd. The Devil with James Bond.** Collins Fontana Books
    1967 1st edition in G.B. Wraps. (First published by John Knox
    Press, U.S.A. 1966)

30007E21 **The New York Times Book Review** Section 7 31 July 1966 p8.
    Pre-publication comment by Lewis Nicholls on 'The Devil with
    James Bond'

    (*See also* 9007J1 **James Bond in Thunderball**
           23007A20 **The James Bond Annual.**)

31007A1 Arthur M. Schlesinger, Jr. A Thousand Days. John F. Kennedy in the White House. Andre Deutsch Ltd. 5th impr May 1967. (1st edn. U.K. Nov 1965). Brief references pp95 + 630. 'His wife does not remember him reading novels except for two or three Ian Fleming thrillers . . . . His supposed addiction to James Bond was partly a publicity gag.'

31007A2 Colin Watson. Licence to Kill. Eyre + Spottiswoode 1971 1st edn. pp233-251.

31007A3 Eric Quayle. The Collector's Book of Detective Fiction. Studio Vista 1972 1st edn. p113. Colour photograph of four Richard Chopping James Bond dustwrappers (and books) pp120-121 re first editions. (States that the name James Bond was first used by Agatha Christie for her unwilling sleuth in The Rajah's Emerald (1934) and, incorrectly, that the majority of James Bond books were also issued in signed limited editions of a few hundred copies which now fetch up to £100 each.

31007A4 Richard Deacon. A History of the Russian Secret Service. Book Club edition (1st published by Frederick Muller Ltd 1972) p430. (includes references to James Bond novels being taken very seriously by Russian Intelligence and to A. Gulyaski who wrote a book in which the communist hero defeated James Bond – *See also* 32007A11)

31007A5 Liverpool Bibliographical Society. Members Exhibition. University of Liverpool July-September 1975 Catalogue. pp1-3. (Items from Collection of Iain Campbell)

31007A6 Another copy of 31007A5 with variant wraps (colour)

31007A7 Joseph Connolly. Collecting Modern First Editions. Studio Vista 1977 pp47-8, 65 Ian Fleming. 1st edition of Casino Royale in dustwrapper is illustrated on front dustwrapper.

31007A8 Paperbacks in Print Winter 1966 J. Whitaker & Sons (Reference Books) Ltd. Lists Pan paperbacks except For Your Eyes Only (presumably temporarily out of print), The Man With the Golden Gun and Octopussy and The Living Daylights (both first printed 1966), and The Spy Who Loved Me (the last James Bond story to be published as a paperback in U.K. in 1967).

31007A9X Daniel N. Fader. Hooked on Books. Pergamon Press 1969 pp52-53, re school library and James Bond Books.

32007A1	**The Twentieth Century** March 1958 pp220-228. Bernard
Bergonzi: The Case of Mr Fleming. Reference also on front wrap.
(Pearson 304, Bond Affair 15, 149, Gant 123-4, Amis 84)

32007A2	**Saturday Review** 26 May 1962 (U.S.A.) p37. Hollis Alpert: 'The
Ian Fleming?' (+ photograph)

32007A3	**The Spectator** 8 June 1962 p744. Spectator's Notebook. Denun-
ciation of James Bond in Soviet Press (Konsomolskaya Pravda)

32007A4	**London Magazine** Vol 2 No 4 July 1962 pp67-70. James Price:
Our Man in the Torture Chamber. (Review of James Bond novels)

32007A5X	**The Spectator** 28 June 1963 p831. Spectator's Notebook.
Criticism of inaccuracies in James Bond Books. (*See* 11007E3 for
reply re Pol Roger champagne)

[32007A600	**Snakes Alive.** Trinity 1963 (Belfast Medical School) Bob Glass.
'The Gunnery of James Bond' (Amis 117-8. *See also* 21007A18)]

32007A7	**The New York Times Book Review** Section 7. 7 June 1964 pp7
and 24. Anthony Boucher: 'There's a Spy Between the Covers'
(references to Fleming + photograph)

32007A8	**The Twentieth Century** Autumn 1964 pp87-88. Brief reference
to James Bond in article 'America's new sexual idols' by Herbert
J. Gans.

32007A9	**Rogue.** April 1965 (U.S.A.) pp26-28, 64, 79. Martin Maloney:
'Ian Fleming: Alice in Nastyland'.

32007A10	**The New York Times Book Review** Section 7. 15 August 1965
p8 Lewis Nicholls: 'The Bond Industry' (on eve of publication in
U.S.A. of The Man With The Golden Gun); also p19 advertisement
for **Gilt Edged Bonds** and **More Gilt Edged Bonds** (*See* 1007D3 +
2007D300)

32007A11	**John O'London's** March 1966 p25. Jacob Faithfull: A rival for
James Bond. (Concerns award winning Bulgarian author Andrei
Gulyashki and his hero Avakoum Zahov, a James Bond of
Eastern Europe, and his views on Bond + Fleming) – *See also*
31007A4

32007A12	**Reader's Digest** February 1966 pp35-39. James Stewart-Gordon:
'007 – The Goldfingered Spy'.

32007A13	**Encounter** May 1966 pp3-6. John Le Carré: 'To Russia With
Greetings' (on front wrap 'Bond in Russia') – an open letter to
the Moscow 'Literary Gazette' re 'The Spy Who Came in from the
Cold' and James Bond.

32007A14	**Playboy** December 1966 pp145 + 343. Kingsley Amis: 'My
Favourite Sleuths' – brief reference to James Bond. Also p3
reference to Fleming re serialisation of Len Deighton's 'An
Expensive Place to Die'.

32007A15	**Exclusive** January 1968 pp12-17. Darrin Scott: 'James Bond
under the Microscope'.

32007A16 **Nova** January 1970 pp2, 3, 6, 7, 9, 12. Mordecai Richter: 'Ian Fleming: a Voice for Little England'. Illustrated by Barrie Tucker.

32007A17 **The Observer** 16 January 1972. Business Observer Section pp11-12. Roger Eglin and Iain Murray: '007 The Gilt Edged Bond' (concerning 'the Bond business's \$700 million income) + Photographs.

32007H18 **Misdaad Loowt Een Enkele Keer** 6 April 1973 pp15-16. Paul Jacobs on Ian Fleming's works.

See also 6007K3 The Spectator 12 October 1962

33007A1   **James Robert Parish (Ed.). The Great Movie Series.** A.S. Barnes & Co. Inc. (U.S.A.) and Thomas Yoseloff Ltd (London) 1971. pp195-208 chapter entitled 'James Bond' (illus.), photo of Sean Connery prominently on front of dustwrapper.

33007A2   **John Brosnan. James Bond in the Cinema.** The Tantivy Press 1972 1st edition.

33007A3   **Brian Davis. The Thriller.** Studio Vista/Dutton Picturebook 1973. Wraps. 1st edition (also published in hardback). References to James Bond films pp42-44, 53-4, 91, 93.

[33007A400 **Emma Andrews. The Films of Sean Connery.** B.C.W. Publishing Ltd. 1974.]

33007A5   **Emma Andrews. The Films of Sean Connery.** B.C.W. Publishing Ltd. 2nd edn. May 1977. Wraps.

33007A6   **007 James Bond in Focus.** Wraps. (Purnell Sept 1964?) Illustrated. Films of **Dr No, From Russia With Love** and **Goldfinger.**

33007A7   **007 James Bond in Focus.** 33007A6 substantially bound in orange cloth.

33007A8   **Steve Blake. Sex And The Starlet.** Merit Books, Chicago, 1965. Wraps. 'Special Illustrated Edition'. pp87-101 relate mainly to 'James Bond's Girls'.

33007E9   **Today** 13 July 1963 pp16-18. Mike Tomies: 'The Secret Life of 007', headed 'When "James Bond" delivered the Milk' – re Sean Connery. Illustrated.

33007E10   **Photoplay** December 1963 p9. Full colour photograph of Sean Connery as James Bond.

33007E11   **Movie + TV Fan-Fare** January 1964 (U.S.A.) Vol 1 No 1 pp22, 23, 54. T. Smith: 'Is Hollywood Safe for 007 Now' – re Sean Connery. Illustrated.

33007E12   **Photoplay** February 1964 pp32-3. 'Bond – Eunice Gayson (Sylvia in the Bond Films) talks to Peter Wright'. Illustrated.

33007E13   **Tit-Bits** 20 June 1964 pp20-21. 'Bond's Wife Hits the Jackpot' – re Diane Cilento and re Eunice Gayson's failure to obtain a part in the third Bond film. Illustrated.

33007E14   **Playboy** November 1965 pp75-84. Playboy Interview – 'Sean Connery'. Illustrated. pp132-143 + front cover James Bond's Girls. Pictorial Essay by Richard Maibaum (scriptwriter of Bond films) – photographs from film stills and of girls in varying stages of undress.

33007E15   **Uncensored** (U.S.A.) February 1966 pp22-3, 53-4. Mabel Ryan-Davies: 'How "James Bond" is rubbing off on Sean Connery'. (Lacks front wrap)

See 24007A11 Playboy July 1966

33007E16   **Daily Express** 30 July 1967 p15. Roderick Mann: '007 Hits the Trail for the Wild West'. (Sean Connery in Shalako + James Bond Films.) (pp5-6 + 15-16 only)

33007E17 **Weekend** 9-15 July 1969 pp20-21, 'Licensed to put on Weight'. Article on Sean Connery and The Red Tent, with photographs of and references to James Bond films.

33007E18 **Cinema X** Vol 2 No 7 n.d. (c1970) p6. 'Sean Connery Talks to Cinema X'.

33007E19 **Parade** 26 August 1972 pp16-17. Peter Mann: 'You've never seen Sean Connery like this before. What James Bond did for Fifteen Bob an Hour'. (re his art class model days)

33007E20 **Cinema X** Vol 4 No 3. n.d. (c1972) pp12-15. 'Connery 007 Birds (again)'. Photographs.

33007E21 **Sunday Express** 13 January 1974 p2. Town Talk gossip column article 'Bernard Lee's New Love', with reference to his playing 'M' in James Bond films. (pp1-2, 31-2 only)

33007E22 **Look In** 8 February 1975 pp14-18. 'Roger Moore as James Bond' with double page colour photograph of Roger Moore.

33007E23 **Knave** Vol 7 No 11 1975 p9. 'It can't be James Bond' (re Roger Moore)

33007E24 **Daily Mail** 22 December 1975 p13. Mail Diary article 'Now Harry Salzman sells his £20m slice of James Bond'. (Sale of 50% of Eon Productions Ltd to United Artists.)

33007E25 **Men Only** November 1976 pp33-34, 36. Interview: 'Sean Connery' by Clarke Taylor, referred to on front wraps as 'Sean Connery's Good Old, Bad Old Bondage'. Another article referred to on front wrap as 'Titti Titti Bang Bang — The Real Russian Revolution'.

33007E26 **Sunday Times Weekly Review** 29 May 1977 p33. Article on Cannes Film Festival with photograph of Roger Moore in front of James Bond film poster (pp33-34 only)

33007L27 **James Bond 007 All Plastic Assembly Kit.** Aurora Kit No 414 in Box 13 x 5¼ x 2¼ inches, with 4pp instructions in French and English. © 1966 Glidrose Productions Ltd + Eon Productions Ltd and Aurora Plastics Corp. (Based on Sean Connery)

33007L28 **Financial Times** 22 July 1976. Nigel Carson: 'Collectively Canned'. (On new U.S. fad of beer can collecting. During 1960s an Arizona brewer produced 'James Bond 007 Special Blend' with pictures of exotically beautiful women on the can which was test marketed and then withdrawn. A single can now fetches $200 on the collectors market.)

(*See also*   9007J1   **James Bond in Thunderball**
           11007K1   **Films and Filming** p5-7 Harry Salzman
                       interview
           24007A11 **Playboy** July 1966)

34007A1　**Lord Strang. Home and Abroad.** Andre Deutsch 1956 1st edn. Contains a full account of Metropolitan-Vickers engineers trial in Moscow 1933 (Fleming's first major success in reporting as a journalist − Pearson 58-71)

34007A2　**Derrick Goodman. Villainy Unlimited.** Elek Books Ltd. 1957. 1st edn. ('the truth about the French underworld to-day') − a little different from the version given by Fleming in his novels, notably Casino Royale and On Her Majesty's Secret Service.

34007A3　**James Bond. Birds of the West Indies.** Collins 1960 (no edition stated). Colour illustrations by Don R. Eckelberry and line drawings by Earl L. Poole. Fleming took the name of his hero from the author of this book. (*See* 26007A17)

34007A4　**J. Bernard Hutton. School for Spies.** Neville Spearman. 1961. 1st edn. Presentation inscription from author on half title page. (*See* 30007A16 re Fleming + Hutton)

34007A5　**John Scarne. Scarne's Complete Guide to Gambling.** Simon and Schuster. New York. 5th Printing. (First published 1961) Fountain of information of the type which Fleming liked to put in his novels − Bond read Scarne on Cards before defeating Drax (Moonraker 32)

34007A6　**Ronald Seth. The Executioners.** The Story of SMERSH. Cassell + Co Ltd. 1967. 1st edn. (True background stories)

34007A7　**Observer Colour Supplement.** 13 May 1973 pp22-23 and cover colour photograph. 'Is this the real James Bond' − re Dusko Popov.

1.   (1007H) Too Hot to Handle is quoted as an additional title by Fleming on verso of half title of 1007D3 which contains Casino Royale!

2.   (5007B1) The Uncorrected Proof Copy is in this instance literally uncorrected. The half title, title page, contents page, Author's Note and pagination are all changed by the first edition. There are over thirty minor textual changes made in Chapter 1, and this pattern is repeated throughout the book. Amongst the more interesting textual changes are the substitution of less offensive asterisks for the first three vowels in Yebionna at the start of Chapter 6 (p53), and the inclusion of the paragraph describing the flight of Tatiana from Rosa Klebb at the end of p90; the paragraph does not appear in the proof copy, which thus makes it seem likely that Tatiana succumbed to the advances about to be made to her.

   Bond also changes his honey on p102 from the original Mount Hymettus to Norwegian Heather (but both bought at Fortnum's); perhaps flying near Mount Hymettus on p120 put him off its honey. This is compensated by Nash losing the brand of what was originally a Dunhill lighter on p221, possibly because he would not have had the same lighter as in his old role as Grant on p13.

   On p239 the bullet fired at Bond travels two yards, compared with the original five yards (an impossibly large compartment even for the ancient rolling stock of the Orient Express ?). On p247 Bond increases his earlier vodka dry Martini to a double vodka Martini; perhaps the reason for him seeing the tip of Rosa Klebb's knife blade on p252 as bluish instead of previously as yellowish.

3.   (12007A1, 13007A1) You Only Live Twice is the only James Bond novel which ends with the words 'The End' instead of a printer's device. (Live And Let Die has neither due to lack of space on the last page.) You Only Live Twice and The Man With The Golden Gun are the only novels which do not have plain endpapers; the design on the endpapers is larger than the endpapers themselves in both cases, which results in the endpaper design apparently varying a little from copy to copy. (This also applies to Octopussy and The Living Daylights.)

4.   (14007D1) The first edition has some minor textual variations from the Sunday Times publication; it also changes the first piece of music played by the orchestra from the original Moussorgsky's Overture to Boris Godunov to the Polovtsian Dances from Prince Igor on p84, possibly making it a Prince Igor evening (see p87). The original unforgivable printing error of 077 is of course corrected to 007 on p93. The Argosy version corresponds with the original Sunday Times version, apart from some minor U.S. spelling variations and the correction of the 077 error.

5.   (14007D3-4) The Playboy version corresponds with the first edition apart from minor U.S. spelling variations.

36. ## AN INDEX
OF SOME PERIODICAL REFERENCES TO
IAN FLEMING
(NOT IN COLLECTION)

American Scholar, Spring 1965
Argosy (U.S.A.), December 1961
The Auk, 1964
Book Week, 20 Nov 1966
Catholic World, June 1965
Commentary, July 1967
Corriera d'informazione, 12 Aug 1964
Corriera della sera, 6 Feb 1965
Current Biography, Oct 1964
La domenica del corriere, No 6, 1965
Esquire, March 1966
L'Espress, 15-21 Feb 1965
L'Espresso, 17 Jan 1965, 31 Jan 1965
L'Express, 22 Aug 1964, 12-18 Oct 1964
L'Europeo, 31 Jan 1965, 7 Mar 1965, 14 Mar 1965
La Fiera Letteraria, 24 Jan 1965
Illustrated London News, 22 Aug 1964
Innostannaya Litteratura, IV, 1966
Journal of Popular Culture, Fall 1967
Ladies Home Journal, Oct 1966
Life, 28 Aug 1964, 2 Nov 1964, 7 Oct 1964, 14 Oct 1964
Listener, LXXIII 788 1965, LXXVI 733-4 1965
Narodna Kultura 22 Apr 1966
New Republic, 30 May 1964
New Statesman, 5 Apr 1958, 30 Mar 1964, 2 Apr 1965, 4 June 1965
New York Herald Tribune, 24 Jan 1965
New York Times, 13 Aug 1964, 23 Feb 1965, 15 Apr 1965, 19 Dec 1965
New Yorker, 21 Apr 1961, 21 Apr 1962
Newsweek, 30 June 1958, 24 Aug 1964, 19 Apr 1965
Le Nouvel Observateur, 18 Feb 1965, 25 Feb 1965
Novyi Mir, IV, 1966
The Observer, 30 May 1965, 23 Oct 1966
Opera Aperta, Jan 1965
Playboy, Mar 1960, Dec 1964, June 1965
Rinascita, 23 Jan 1965
Rogue, Feb 1961
Saturday Review, 7 Aug 1965
Show, Nov 1964
South Atlantic Quarterly, Winter 1967
Sports Illustrated, 24 May 1965
La Stampa, No 50, 1965
Studies Journal (Univ of Kansas), Fall 1965
Time, 5 May 1965

The Times, 26 Mar, 30 Oct 1952, 7 Apr, 31 Dec 1954, 11 Apr 1957, 3 Apr
    1958, 26 Mar 1959, 21 Apr, 3 Oct, 10 Dec 1960, 25 Mar, 30 Mar, 22 Apr,
    16 Sept 1961, 19 Apr 1962, 4 Apr, 18, 21-23, 26-30 Nov, 4 Dec 1963,
    19 Mar, 13, 18, 19 Aug, 16 Sept, 10 Nov, 1 Dec 1964, 1 Apr, 30 Aug, 30
    Sept, 8, 11, 19, 28 Oct 1965, 22 Feb, 16 Aug, 20 Aug, 3 Sept, 27 Oct,
    15 Dec 1966, 10 Apr, 8 May, 7 July 1967, 5 Jan, 30 Mar, 1 June, 14 Dec
    1968, 2 Jan, 15 Sept 1969, 18 Dec 1971, 27 Sept 1972
The Times Literary Supplement, 23 June 1961, 12 May 1965, 27 May 1965,
    27 Oct 1966
Vogue (U.S.A.), Mar 1954
Vogue, Sept 1965
Zeit, 20 Mar 1964

Many newspapers and periodicals published articles especially at the time of
the Thunderball Lawsuit (end Nov 1963), of the author's death (12 August
1964) and of the United Artists film premicres (Oct 1962, Oct 1963, Sept
1964, Dec 1965, July 1967, etc.). Many of the books were serialised in the
Daily Express, which also had a James Bond cartoon strip for many years
(briefly revived in Sunday Express in 1977). The bulk of Fleming's journalism
is of course contained in Sunday Times, in which he wrote articles from 1949
onwards and in which he wrote the Atticus column from October 1953
onwards.

APPENDIX 2

37. LIST OF REFERENCES RELATING TO FLEMING IN THE SPECTATOR 1950-1966

[18 Aug 1950	211	Spectator Competition No 33 Set by Fleming.]
15 Sept 1950	290	Report by Fleming on Competition No 33.
17 Apr 1953	494	Book Review: Casino Royale. R.D. Charques.
22 Apr 1955	512	Book Review: Moonraker. John Metcalf.
5 Aug 1955	199-200	Book Review by Fleming of Erskine Childers: The Riddle of the Sands.
12 Aug 1955	220	Letters re Fleming Book Review.
23 Dec 1955	862-3	His Word, His Bond by I*N FL*M*NG.
6 Apr 1956	446	Advert: Diamonds Are Forever.
	462, 464	Book Review: Diamonds Are Forever. John Russell.
12 Apr 1957	493	Book Review: From Russia With Love. Anthony Hartley.
13 Dec.1957	40	Advert: The Diamond Smugglers.
		Book Review: The Diamond Smugglers. Dan Jacobson.
4 Apr 1958	424-5	Automobilia. Article by Fleming.
	438	Book Review: Dr No. Simon Raven.
[11 Apr 1958	460	Letters re Automobilia.]
27 Mar 1959	448	Book Review: Goldfinger. Christopher Pym.
9 Oct 1959	466-7	If I Were Prime Minister. Article by Fleming.
16 Oct 1959	520	Letters re If I Were Prime Minister.
12 Feb 1960	207	Thrilling Cities: 32781 Queen of the North West. By I–N FL–M––G. Bernard Levin.
29 Apr 1960	635	Book Review: For Your Eyes Only. Christopher Pym.
31 Mar 1961	452	Book Review: Thunderball. Geoffrey Grigson.
1 June 1962	728-9	Book Review: The Spy Who Loved Me. Esther Howard.
8 June 1962	744	Spectators Notebook: – denunciation of James in Soviet Press.
12 Oct 1962	549	Spectators Notebook: – film of Dr No
	557	Letter 'Russian Bonds'.
	560	Film Review: Dr No. Ian Cameron.
26 Oct 1962	636	Letter from Fleming.
26 Apr 1963	540	Advert: On Her Majesty's Secret Service.
	544	Book Review: On Her Majesty's Secret Service. Antonia Sandford.
[28 June 1963	831	Spectator's Notebook: – inaccuracies in James Bond books.]
19 July 1963	82	Letter re 'inaccuracy' in James Bond book.
[18 Oct 1963	495-6	Film Review: From Russia With Love. Isobel Quigly.]
20 Dec 1963	827-8	Book Review: Thrilling Cities. Dom Moraes,

20 Mar 1964	385	Advert: You Only Live Twice.
	389	Book Review: You Only Live Twice. Simon Raven.
18 Sept 1964	372	Film Review: Goldfinger. Isobel Quigly.
2 Oct 1964	444-5	Book Review: Double 0 Seven James Bond: A Report by O.F. Snelling. Simon Raven.
2 Apr 1965	447	Book Review: The Man With the Golden Gun. Simon Raven.
7 May 1965	605	Advert: Serialisation of The James Bond Dossier in the Daily Mirror.
28 May 1965	694-5	Book Review: The James Bond Dossier by Kingsley Amis. Simon Raven.
11 June 1965	753	Letter re The James Bond Dossier.
[31 Dec 1965	864-5	Film Review: Thunderball. Isobel Quigley.]
8 July 1966	50, 52	Book Review: Octopussy and The Living Daylights. Simon Raven.
	51	Advert: Octopussy and The Living Daylights.
28 Oct 1966	552-3	Book Review/Article: The Life of Ian Fleming by John Pearson. Simon Raven.

(A guide to the type of coverage Fleming received from a serious periodical, admittedly possibly a little prejudiced in his favour since Peter Fleming wrote for the Spectator from 1931 onwards.)

[   ] signifies not in collection.

Argosy (U.K.), Feb 1962, 3D
Argosy (U.S.A.), June 1962, 14D
Bibliography in Britain 3, 1964, 27a, 4, 1965, 27a
The Book Collector, Spring 1952, 22A, Winter 1964, 27A, Spring 1965, 27A
Book Collecting and Library Monthly, Jan 1969, 24E
The Bookman, Nov 1960, 21A
Books and Bookmen, Mar 1959, 7E, Apr 1959, 7E
The Bookseller, 30 Dec 1967, 23a
British Books, Sept 1964, 27A
British Ski Year Book, 1963, 11E
Cinema X, Vol 1 No 12, 12K, Vol 2 No 7 33E, Vol 4 No 5 33F
The Companion, No 205, 23F
Courier, Apr 1964, 17E, Apr 1965, 9K
Daily Express, 30 July 1967, 33E, 7 Mar 1968, 23K, 30 May 1970, 23K, 11
    Feb 1971, 23K, 14 Oct 1971, 23K, 18 May 1972, 23K, 4 Nov 1974, 24A,
    16, 17, 18, 19, 20 Dec 1974, 13J, 14 Oct 1975, 29A
Daily Mail, 22 Dec 1975, 33E
Daily Mirror, 6 Dec 1976, 10K
Dapper, Apr 1965, 7K
Encounter, Jan 1965, 27A, May 1966, 32A
Exclusive, Jan 1968, 32A
Films and Filming, Oct 1964, 7K, July 1967, 12K, Sept 1969, 11K
Films Illustrated, Sept 1973, 4K
Financial Times, 22 July 1976, 33L
The Guardian, 3 Mar 1977, 29A
Harvard Lampoon, 24A
Horizon, Dec 1947, 21A
The Horn Book Magazine, Apr 1965, 18E
Investor's Chronicle, 13 Aug 1976, 29A
John O'London's, 25 Feb 1960, 16E, 11 Oct 1962, 6K, Mar 1966, 32A,
    Apr 1966, 9K
The Junior Bookshelf, Feb 1965, 18E
Kinematograph Weekly, 14 Dec 1968, 18K
Knave, Vol 7 No 11 1975, 33E
Life, 17 Mar 1961, 5E
Life International, 24 Sept 1962, 27A, 2 Nov 1964, 7K
Life and Letters, July 1931, 22A
Lilliput, May-June 1953, 1E, June 1955, 3E, May 1959, 7E
The Listener, 14 Nov 1963, 17E, 26 Mar 1964, 12E, 14 July 1966, 14F,
    28 Mar 1968, 23E
Look, 15 Nov 1966, 1K
Look in, 8 Feb 1975, 33E
London Magazine, May 1956, 4e, Dec 1959, 21A, July 1962, 32A, Apr 1963,
    24A, June 1965, 30E, Oct 1966, 26E
Mayfair, Vol 9 No 5, 2J, Vol 9 No 7, 12K
Men Only, Nov 1976, 33F
Men's Digest, June 1966, 24A
Misdead Loont een Enkele Keer, 6 Apr 1973, 32H

Movie + T.V. Fanfare, Jan 1964, 33E
New Statesman (and Nation), 9 May 1953, 1E, 14 Apr 1956, 4E, 27 Apr
   1957, 5E, 11 May 1962, 10E, 5 Apr 1963, 11E, 8 Oct 1965, 20E, 28 Oct
   1966, 26E, 7 Jan 1972, 4K, 1 July 1977, 23E
New York Times Book Review, 28 Oct 1956, 4E, 22 June 1958, 16E, 7 June
   1964, 32A, 25 July 1965, 30E, 15 Aug 1965, 32A, 22 Aug 1965, 13E,
   31 July 1966, 30E, 11 Dec 1966, 26E
Newsweek, 6 May 1958, 23E
Nova, Jan 1970, 32A
Now + Then, Spring 1961, 9D, Autumn 1960, 28A
The Observer, 16 Jan 1972, 32A
The Observer Colour Magazine, 6 Sept 1964, 7K, 31 Mar 1968, 23K, 13 May
   1973, 34A
Parade, 26 Aug 1972, 33E
Photoplay, Dec 1963, 33E, Feb 1964, 33E, Aug 1964, 7K, Dec 1966, 12K
Photoplay Film Monthly, Jan 1970, 11K, June 1971, 4K, Sept 1971, 4K,
   Mar 1972, 4K, April 1977, 10K
Playboy, April, May, June 1963, 11D, July 1963, 11d, Jan 1964, 15D, April,
   May, June 1964, 12D, Dec 1964, 21A, April, May, June, July 1965, 13D,
   Nov 1965, 33E, March, April 1966, 14D, July, August 1966, 24A, Dec
   1966, 24a, 32A
Private Eye, 14 Apr 1967, 24A
Punch, 6 May 1953, 1E, 14 April 1954, 2E, 27 April 1955, 3E, 13 Nov 1957,
   24A, 18 July 1962, 28A, 20 Feb 1963, 29A, 23 Oct 1963, 5K, 30 Sept
   1964, 7K, 9 Mar 1966, 24A
Reader's Digest, Feb 1966, 32A, Aug 1966, 26D
Rex, No 9 1973, 2J
Rogue, Apr 1965, 32A
Saturday Review, 26 May 1962, 32A, 7 Nov 1964, 18E, 12 Dec 1964, 7K
Scene, 5 Oct 1962, 6K
Screen International, 14 Jan 1978, 8J
Snakes Alive, Trinity, 1963, 32A
Stag, May 1962, 6D
Sunday Express, 31 Jan 1971, 19e, 13 Jan 1974, 33E, 3 Feb 1974, 29A,
   7 July 1974, 13K, 15 Aug 1976, 10K, 31 Oct 1976, 10K
Sunday Telegraph, 2, 9, 16, 23 Sept 1973, 23K
Sunday Times, 25 Nov 1973, 5C
Sunday Times Colour Section/Magazine, 4 Feb 1962, 12D, 18 Nov 1962, 21A,
   23 Nov 1969, 29A, 23 Jan 1971, 29A
Sunday Times Weekly Review, 29 May 1977, 33E
The Tablet, 23 Apr 1955, 3E, 25 Apr 1959, 7E, 30 Apr 1960, 8E, 29 Apr
   1961, 9E, 28 Apr 1962, 10E, 25 Apr 1964, 12E
The Tatler + Bystander, 27 Nov 1963, 17E
Time, 10 Apr 1964, 5K, 21 Aug 1964, 27A
Time and Tide, 10 Aug 1967, 12K
The Times, 18 Mar 1939, 21A, 24, 25, 27, 28 Mar 1939, 21A, 21 Nov 1973,
   15C, 27 Dec 1973, 29A, 17 Dec 1974, 28a, 20 Dec 1974, 13X, 4, 6, 14
   Oct 1975, 29A, 7 Jan 1976, 29A, 4 Nov 1976, 29A, 28 Mar 1977, 10K
The Times Literary Supplement, 20 Apr 1962, 10E
Tit-Bits, 20 June 1964, 33E
Today, 13 July 1963, 33E
TV Times, 30 Oct 1976, 7K, 5 Nov 1977, 24A
The Twentieth Century Magazine, Mar 1958, 32A, May 1959, 7E, Aug 1960,
   8E, Autumn 1964, 32A

Uncensored, Feb 1966, 33E
Weekend, 9 July 1969, 33E

(Note: The reference numbers have been abbreviated and consist here of the pre-007 prefix and the suffix immediately after 007 only; thus 3007D2 is abbreviated to 3D.)

(*See also* Appendix 2, The Spectator.)

39. INDEX OF PERSONS (NON-FICTIONAL)

Adams, Maud, 13K
Adams, Tom, 23A,a,C
Allen, Woody, 1K
Alpert, Hollis, 7K, 32A
Ambler, Eric, 5C, 8D, 29A
Amis, Kingsley, 23A,C,E,F, 30A,B,E, 30,G,H, 32A
Andress, Ursula, 6J, 24A
Andrews, Emma, 33A
Anne, Princess, 10J
Antonini, Fausto, 30A
Armour, Tommy, 4C
Armstrong, Neil, 29A
Atkinson, Alex, 24A

Bach, Barbara, 10K
Baker, J. Roger, 17E
Barbato, Andrea, 30A
Barkham, John, 16E
Barsley, Michael, 5C, 30A
Baumfield, Brian, 7E
Bell, Marty, 24A
Benson, David, 9J
Bergonzi, Bernard, 32A
Biggs-Davison, John, 3E
Blackman, Honor, 7J, 7K
Blake, Steve, 33A
Blofeld, Rev Thomas Calthorpe 11C
Bond, James (ornithologist), 20A
Bond, Mary Wickham, 20A, 26E
Boothroyd, J.B., 3E
Borgonelli, Isobella, 24A
Bottome, Phyllis, 22A
Boucher, Anthony, 1d, 4E, 13E, 32A
Boyd, Ann S., 30A,E
Braddon, Russell, 29A
Bremner, Marjorie, 7E, 8E
Broccoli, Albert R., 18J
Brophy, Brigid, 11E
Brooke-Smith, W.P., 21E
Brosnan, John, 33A
Bryce, Ivar, 26A
Burgess, Anthony, 14E
Burke, John, 18J
Burningham, John, 18A,a,F,G,H

Calisi, Romano, 30A
Cameron, Ian, 6K

Campbell, Alexander, 12C
Campbell, Iain, 31A
Cargill, Morris, 20A
Carson, Nigel, 33A
Carter, Ernestine, 22A
Carter, John, 22A
Chamberlain, Christopher, 23A
Chambers, Dave, 18a
Chandler, Raymond, 21A, 30A
Charques, R.D., 1E
Cheetham, Anthony, 24A
Childers, Erskine, 21A
Chopping, Richard, 5A,F, 7A, 8A, 9A, 10A, 11A, 12A, 13A, 14A, 30A, 31A
Chrichard, 13F
Christie, Agatha, 31A
Christie, Ian, 13J
Cilento, Diane, 29A, 33E
Clark, Jim, 29A
Clavell, James, 21A
Clemens, M.B., 23D
Coleman, John, 4K
Coleman, Roger, 13D
Colombo, Furio, 30A
Connery, Sean, 4J, 7K, 9J, 10K, 12D, 12J, 24A, 30A, 33A, 33E
Connolly, Cyril, 24A,E, 26E
Connolly, Joseph, 31A
Cooper, Gary, 25A
Coward, Noel, 22A
Crawley, Tony, 9J
Culbertson, Ely, 3C
Cuthill, 7F, 8F, 9F, 10F, 11F, 12F

Dahl, Roald, 12K
Darroll, Aedwyn, 20A
Davis, Paul, 17A
De Gaulle, General, 24A
De La Lanne Mirrlees, Robin, 11C,c
Deacon, Richard, 31A
Deighton, Len, 25A, 29A, 30A, 32A
Del Buono, Oreste, 30A
Diment, Adam, 25A
Downie, R.A., 30A
Dulles, Allen, 13B, 29A, 30A

Eaton, Shirley, 7K

68

Eckelberry, Don R., 34A
Eco, Umberto, 30A
Edwards, Hugh, 20A,a
Eglin, Roger, 32A
Enright, D.J., 23E
Evans, Peter, 30A
Ewart, Gavin, 30A

Fader, David N., 31A
Faithfull, Jacob, 32A
Feck, Lou, 14D
Ferguson, Ken, 7K
ffolkes, 5K
Fishman, Jack, 30A
Fleming, Anne, 19e
Fleming, Caspar, 29A
Fleming, Major David, 29A
Fleming, Ian (artist), 24A
Fleming, Lucy, 22A
Fleming, Peter, 1D, 22A, 28A, 29A
Forster, Klim, 23D
Forsyth, Frederick, 25A
Foster, Larry, 24A
Fraser, Eric, 20A

Gallico, Paul, 1D
Galton, Ray, 24A
Gans, Herbert J., 32A
Gant, Richard, 26A
Gardner, John, 25A
Gayson, Eunice, 33E
Gilchrist, Roderick, 10K
Gilmour, Ian, 24A
Glaite, 18H
Glass, Bob, 32A
Glass, Douglas, 7E
Gloag, John, 21E
Goldman, Albert, 26E
Goodman, Derrick, 34A
Gordon, Gwen, 18A
Graves, Charles, 22A
Gray, Rod, 24H
Green, Peter, 6K
Green, Tim, 27A
Greene, Grahame, 1D
Greene, Hugh, 1D
Grigson, Geoffrey, 9E
Gris, Henry, 30A
Gulyaski, Andrei, 31A, 32A

Hailsham, Lord, 24A
Hall, William, 4J, 12K
Hamilton, Iain, 24A
Hamlisch, Marvin, 10K

Hana, Mie, 12K
Harding, Colin, 7c
Harris, Mel, 22A
Hart-Davis, Duff, 28A
Hartley, Anthony, 5E
Hayward, John, 1b, 22A
Hefner, Hugh M., 8D
Heins, Paul, 18E
Hill, Derek, 6K
Hine, Al, 30E
Hobson, Harold, 28A
Holt, John, 9J
Honig, Louis, 8H
Horak, 23D
Hough, Richard, 3D
Howard, Esther, 10E
Howard, Michael S., 28A,a
Hudson, Lord, 21A,a
Hugh-Jones, Siriol, 17E
Hutton, J. Bernard, 30A, 34A
Hyde, H. Montgomery, 28A

Ingrams, Richard, 24A

Jackson, Dan, 16E
Jacob, Alaric, 22A, 29A
Jacobs, Paul, 32H
Jeller, 14D
Jennings, Betty, 4K
Johns, Ken, 11K
Johnson, Celia, 22A
Jones, D.A.N., 20E
Kemsley, Lord, 20A, 22A
Kennedy, John F., 5E, 31A
Kennedy, Vicki, 7K
Kipling, Rudyard, 23D
Kirkbride, Ronald, 25A
Kirkup, James, 12C
Knightley, Philip, 28A
Knocker, G.M., 21E
Kroger, Peter, 25A

E.L., 4J
Lane, Sheldon, 30A
Larkin, Philip, 14E
Lazenby, George, 11K
Le Carre, John, 32A
Lee, Bernard, 19e, 33E
Legge, Michael, 12K
Leigh-Fermor, Patrick, 2C
Lejeune, Anthony, 7E, 8E, 9E, 10E,
   12E
Levin, Bernard, 24A
Lewin, David, 9J

(Note: The reference numbers have been abbreviated and consist here of the pre-007 prefix and the suffix immediately after 007 only; thus 13007K1 becomes 13K.)

Produced by Comersgate Limited, 30 Cornmarket Street, Oxford.